Ginny®
America's Sweetheart

Published by Hobby House Press, Inc.
Grantsville, Maryland 21536

Hobby
House
Press™

DEDICATIONS

This book would not have been possible without the help of Ann Roberts Tardie. Ann has an incredible working knowledge of the *Ginny* doll market. As a collector, she has assembled a collection of Vogue dolls second to none. My heartfelt thanks go out to this giving, generous person.

A. Glenn Mandeville

ACKNOWLEDGMENTS

A project of this scope could not be accomplished without the help of some very special people. My deepest thanks go to Barbara Bell, Thea Crozier, Gary Fischer, Bob Gantz, Elaine Hydorn, Kathi Van Laar, Kevin Wedman, Judy Traina, Linda Collie and Dick Tahsin

Special thanks to Aura (Gidget) Donnelly for loaning photos of dolls from her fabulous collection. All Donnelly collection dolls photographed by Bettina Stoes. The following photographs are copyrighted by Gidget Donnelly: title page photo, 2, 3.

Front Cover caption: Bobby Soxer. Courtesy Vogue Doll Company. See page 134 for more information.
Title Page caption: 1951 Sports Series *Roller Skater. Gidget Donnelly collection.*
Back Cover caption: 1950-1951 Crib Crowd Series three *Sleep Eye Babies. Gidget Donnelly collection.*

Additional copies of this book may be purchased at $14.95 (plus postage and handling) from

Hobby House Press, Inc.

1 Corporate Drive
Grantsville, Maryland 21536
or from your favorite bookstore or dealer.
or call **1-800-554-1447**. Fax number **301-895-5029**. E-mail: hobbyhouse@gcnet.net

TABLE OF CONTENTS

The Background of Jennie Graves 5

The Early Years of Vogue...8

Painted-Eye Hard Plastic, A New Beginning (1948-50)..............................12

The Golden Years - Experiments And Triumphant Success 21

Now *Ginny* Walks..49

1955-56 — Molded Lashes and Pretty Clothes! 59

1957 On — The End of an Era 71

The 1960s — And Ginny...79

The 1970s — The Story Continues 85

1984 — A New Beginning 90

The Dakin Years...92

Ginny the New Generation 96

Appendix

    A. The Accessories 136

    B. Why Collect *Ginny* Dolls 140

    C. How to Collect *Ginny* Dolls 141

    D. The Care (And Repair!) of *Ginny* 142

    E. An Identification Guide to Vogue Clothing Labels 144

Price Guide 146

Ginny Doll Club 158

Index 159

The Early Years of
VOGUE

In 1922, When the Vogue Doll Shoppe opened, little did Mrs. Graves know that a huge demand existed for her work. Up until that time most dolls had been sold undressed, or dressed in just a chemise or simple outfit. In the 1880s, when the French bébés were being imported into this country, fancy dresses and hats abounded from the latest Paris fashions. As the German doll makers began to force an end to the reign of the French dolls (through lower prices), quality suffered in the area of costuming.

Mrs. Graves believed that the clothing on a doll could really make a difference, and began designing clothes for bisque dolls which she imported. Eventually she turned to the Just Me dolls from Germany, manufactured by Armand Marseille. She used both the 8in (20.3cm) size, and the 10in (25.4cm) model, using poodle cut wigs and importing trunks which were used to create entire gift sets for the dolls. Today, we can identify these Just Me dolls as they are made of either fired bisque, or painted bisque, with fine sleep-eyes. Marked "Just Me/Registered/Germany" with various numbers, they are easy to verify. Some of the outfits from this late 1920s-early

2. A composition bent leg *Sunshine Baby* from the 1940s, mint-in-box complete with sticker. *Gidget Donnelly collection.*

3. A Vogue composition *Toddles* with MIB wardrobe that dates circa 1945-49 and has the "Ink Blot" tag. *Gidget Donnelly collection.*

1930s period have a small white cotton tag with "VOGUE" sewn in gold attached to the garment. The shoes are fine leatherette, and tie, with little pompons attached. Clothing styles are similar to those on the *Patsy* series by Effanbee, all of which mirrored childrens' fashions of the period.

The collector of these early dolls will still be able to find examples in original clothes. They were almost too cute to play with, and many surface from time to time in flawless mint condition. It is not known with any certainty if names were assigned to any of the dolls, but it appears that the ones this author has examined that were still in the original boxes, did not. The boxes are plain cardboard lined with paper doilies,

Mrs. Graves believed that the clothing on a doll could really make a difference.

and just marked "Made in Germany" on the end of the box.

As the situation worsened between the United States and Germany, it became increasingly more difficult to find these dolls to dress. Soon it became unpatriotic as well to buy German imports, and Mrs. Graves was faced with a new problem...where to find dolls to dress in her fabulous designs.

The Appeal of the *Just Me* doll encouraged Mrs. Graves try to find a sculptor and a company that could produce a similar doll in the newest medium for doll making, composition. Soon Mrs. Graves' search led her to Bernard Lipfert, the leading sculptor of doll heads. Mr. Lipfert had done most of the *Patsy* heads for Effanbee, and Ideal had commissioned him for such dolls as *Shirley Temple*. Mr. Lipfert's designs had an identifiable "look" as can be seen in the similarities between *Patsyette* and the composition doll Vogue eventually marketed.

> *Vogue was one of the first small manufacturers to make composition dolls.*

This part of the business was very new to Mrs. Graves. She had been used to simply ordering dolls and dressing them. Now she suddenly found herself in the position of making dolls as well. Soon, however, she was able to find a company willing to manufacture a composition doll, using her molds and meeting her specifications. Composition dolls, with their "Can't Break-em" advertising (first started by Horsman and Effanbee), had caught on very fast. This material made from glue, sawdust, and other materials, then baked and painted, freed the doll makers from the fragility of playthings.

Ironically as any collector knows, composition has turned out to be more sus-

ceptible than porcelain to the perils of crazing (surface lines in the paint) and outright cracking, resulting in unsightly breaks in the entire surface. Extremes in temperatures seem to cause the most damage, as dolls stored in hot attics or damp basements seem to have fared the worst. As a natural product, composition absorbs moisture from the air and expands, resulting in fine cracking in the painted surface which does not expand, and when subjected to extreme heat, dries out and splits open. Nonetheless, to a child who usually only required the doll to last a few years, this new medium was welcomed, and resulted in dolls being cheaper, sturdier, and more readily available.

Mrs. Graves became one of the first of the smaller manufacturers to use this new material to its best advantage. In 1937, all her dolls used this composition and continued to do so until 1947-1948.

During this period Virginia Graves Carlson came to work for her mother, and eventually took over as chief designer. Like most companies, Vogue did not keep records of their dolls for very long. They never dreamed that someday the doll would be collected by adults who would want to know everything about how the dolls were made and sold.

New Series such as the "Sunshine Babies" were tried, and had the same heads, torsos and arms, but were made with curved legs. Dressed elaborately, and often marketed in gift sets, they are as beautiful today as when made in the early 1940s.

For a time, when imports became tight, and manufacturing demands impossible, Mrs. Graves purchased dolls from the Arranbee Doll Company. These were marked "R&B" on the back. Later composition dolls were marked "Vogue" on the head, and "Doll Co" on the back. Most of the little girls were called *Toddles* and had this name stamped in ink on the bottom of her shoe. It seemed Mrs. Graves had shied away from naming her dolls, and resorted instead to series names, such as "Nursery Rhyme" dolls, "Fairy Tale" dolls, and "Far-Away Places." Very popular was the military group consisting of *Captain, Sailor, Uncle Sam, Aviator, Nurse* and *Soldier*. Also manufactured was a "Cinderella Group" with *Cinderella, Prince Charming*, and the *Fairy Godmother*. These characters, too, had their series' name stamped in ink on the bottom of their shoes. A later addition was the "Bridal Party," with *Bride, Bridesmaid, Groom*, and *Minister*.

4. A beautiful example of a mint-in-box doll, this *Fairy Godmother*, marked the same as *Mistress Mary*, also her name on her shoes. Her original box adds a great deal to her value. *Author's collection.*

By 1943 Vogue had taken as a slogan, "Fashion Leaders in Doll Society, " and Vogue became incorporated in 1945. Separate clothing was also available for the little *Toddles* dolls. Exciting and imaginative accessories came along for the dolls – such as rakes, bars of soap and towels. Through *Toddles* and the other characters, a child could at last have a sturdy companion. By the end of the 1940s, the best was yet to come, as manufacturing techniques were forever changed by one word ... plastic!

Painted Eye Hard Plastics
A New Beginning
(1948-1950)

Toward the end of World War II a new material had found its place in the American war effort. Developed primarily for use in creating lighter fighter planes, plastics soon began to revolutionize industry. Doll makers, long plagued by the instability of composition, were ecstatic over this new development. For ten years companies had experimented with formulas which wouldn't craze or peel, but the battle could not be won. As long as a natural wood base product was being used, the dampness and heat would expand and contract the material. Vogue's composition dolls seem to develop fine line crazing, but many have survived in perfect condition for today's collectors.

With plastics, the main advantage was that new molds did not have The manufacturers were overjoyed because the quality of their dolls would be improved, while the cost remained the same. Now dolls were

5, 6, 7. In 1950 a series called "One Half Century Group," consisting of seven dolls, were available. Considered today to be among the rarest of all Vogue Dolls, they are all painted-eye hard plastics, except the *Miss 2000*, which had sleep-eyes, to show the progress of the company. Shown here are *Miss 1910*, looking very much from the period, and *Miss 1920*. *Miss 2000* is costumed quite simply, yet conveys the message of a future time. *Barbara Bell collection.*

6

7

8. A ***Brother-Sister*** set is done in tones of blue included with the dolls are these unique accessories consisting of an assortment of gardening tools, a wheelbarrow, and a watering can. *Ann Tardy collection.*

> *By 1949, virtually every manufacturer was using plastic.*

washable! Wigs could be washed on a doll head, and no damage resulted. The new material was a dream come true for the doll industry. By 1949, virtually every manufacturer was using the new plastic medium for their dolls, producing toys which today are virtually indestructible.

Vogue began making adorable sets of twins, dressed in matching outfits as brother and sister, and issued an infant called a Crib

9. This clown is adorable in his taffeta clown suit and hat. The same basic doll as the Brother series, he shows the simple, yet effective costuming designed by Mrs Graves and her daughter. *Ann Tardie collection.*

10. One of the favorite of the storybook characters is this *Red Riding Hood*. She is store-mint in her satin cape. Her organdy flowered dress is labeled, and the basket is original to the doll. This is one of the carry-over dolls from the composition era, as the author has one just like her in composition. *Ann Tardie collection.*

Crowd baby, which even had rubber pants. For 1948, the company experimented with many new names and styles, including holiday specials and theme dolls. Nursery rhymes continued to be popular, and additional boxed outfits could transform each doll into a new plaything. These painted-eye hard plastic dolls are all marked "Vogue" on the head, and "Vogue Doll" on the body. If a doll is not marked, it is not a Vogue Doll from this period.

12. *John Alden* and *Priscilla* of the "Frolicking Fables" series from 1951-52. *Gidget Donnelly collection.*

11. #5 1950 MIB painted eye *Julie. Gidget Donnelly collection.*

13. One of the most collectible series from this period are the Crib Crowd babies. Basically the same doll as the rest, the only difference is her bent-leg baby styling. The clothing is usually labeled, and has fine drawstring threaded through the neckline. Socks tied with ribbons and plastic "rubber" pants complete this baby outfit. Her chair is Vogue, but dates from the mid-1950s. *Author's collection.*

14. Every collector dreams of finding dolls still mint-in-box such as this little girl. Her Mohair wig is auburn, with a mint dress and hat in pink taffeta. Her labeled dress is cotton organdy, similar to *Red Riding Hood*. A perfect treasure in a Vogue box. *Ann Tardie collection.*

These two years, 1948 and 1949, produced a great many treasures that have survived today. The "Golden Era" of dolls, the 1950s was about to begin!

15. A painted eye *Ginny* from the 1950s probably dressed for Easter. *Gidget Donnelly collection.*

16. Representative of the little girl dolls of the period, this doll still has her original foil wrist tag. Her blue dress has an attached white organdy apron. All the dolls from this period has leatherette center snap shoes in various colors. *Ann Tardie collection.*

17. More Crib Crowd babies romping in the nursery. Even these dolls originally came with the silver foil wrist tags. These dolls have somewhat curly wigs, and are originally dressed in tagged outfits. The girl on the left wears a taffeta dress and hat in peach, while the little lady on the right sports a white organdy dress tied at the neck. *Ann Tardie collection.*

18. These two little girls of the period are wearing similar styles in labeled clothing. The doll on the left is wearing a blue taffeta dress and matching panties, while the doll on the right is in pink cotton. Taffeta hair ribbons and leatherette center snap shoes in matching colors complete their ensembles. *Thea Crozier collection.*

19. Mrs. Grave's love of fine millinery is really shown in the lovely hat on this doll. Her dress is of blue cotton, with white lace trim. The hat is a combination of the two fabrics, as were most of the hats of this period, and set off the doll's lovely coloring. *Author's Collection.*

20. This *Sister* needs her Brother. The dolls were sold separately and not as a set, resulting in many separated children. #34, 1952. *Author's Collection.*

The Golden Years
Experiments & Success

By 1950, Vogue Dolls, under the able direction of Mrs. Graves, had moved forward to become one of the leading companies producing 8in (20.3cm) dolls.

The new plastic medium was well suited to being poured into the composition molds. Now, however, companies were discovering that more detail could be achieved than previously thought. New wig materials spawned by the plastics industry were making innovations possible, and even light weight plastic doll eyes were now available, replacing the heavy weighted glass ones, meaning that small dolls could now have the same features as their larger counterparts. Experimentation became the watchword of the 1950s. Plastics had opened the door for new designs; now it was up to clever people to translate these new ideas into exciting dolls.

In 1951 a new doll was available from Vogue. The same size as the painted-eye dolls, she had a new feature, a synthetic wig made of a new miracle fiber, trade-

21. Transitional clothing and materials started of the 1950s. This *Red Riding Hood* has the same outfit as her earlier painted-eye sister. Her eyes are a delicate pastel color rather than the intense color used later on. *Author's collection.*

22. Another "carry-over". From the painted-eye period is *Mistress Mary*. She is all original, and her outfit is untagged. Many outfits from 1951-52 surface untagged. Perhaps the home sewers that year were not provided with as many tags as in previous years. *Author's collection.*

23. This *Easter Bunny* was a holiday special. His special hair is made of the same material as his suit. Collectors consider this a real find! *Ann Tardie collection.*

24. A rare version of a Crib Crowd baby is shown here. Her wig is the same as those used on the painted-eye dolls; her finish, however, and sleep-eyes date her from 1950. This proves over again that materials were used up as new issues came out. *Ann Tardie collection.*

25. By 1951, The Crib Crowd babies and wigs like those used on the "poodle-cut" dolls. Basically this doll is different from a "Poodle" just in the bent baby legs. *Ann Tardie collection.*

marked "Nutex," that could be washed, set, and curled just like real hair. The hair styles could now be changed along with the clothes.

To introduce this feature, dolls were made wearing a plastic shoulder cape, just like a real beauty parlor, to protect her clothing, and came with a round plastic hat box made of acetate that contained little pink curlers. The other big feature of these new dolls was that their tiny eyes opened and closed, and looked as life-like as human eyes. Buyers were ecstatic. This truly was a big break through in doll manufacturing, and would set the trend for the next several years.

Gradually other innovative ideas were tried; plastic eyes made of violet and odd shades of blue appeared. Soon manufacturers learned that even the plastic itself could be painted as was the composition and, for a while, dolls were painted over with a bisque-like finish or a shiny wax-like coating.

Mrs. Graves and daughter Virginia had avoided naming the little girl dolls of the late 1940s. Thinking that a child would like to name her own doll, they were identified on salesman's sheets with stock numbers and a brief description. For reasons still

26. By 1952, the "poodle-cut" wigs were all the rage. Outfits can now be identified by stock numbers from salesmen's catalogs, making identification easier for today's collector. This doll is from the "Kindergarten Series" and is #30. *Ann Tardie collection.*

27. Another mystery for the collector is that the outfits shown in the catalogs were often produced in many colors. This is *Tiny Miss* #41 from 1952, in two colors, red and blue. Each has its own matching leatherette center snap shoes. *Author's collection.*

28. This adorable "Poodle-cut" doll is dressed in the 1952 "Sports Series." It should be noted that in the company catalogs, any doll was shown to illustrate an outfit. The "poodle-cuts" came dressed not just in the outfits pictured, but in all styles illustrated. The same is true for side-parted wigs, and hair colors. Many of these dolls turn up in original boxes, labeled, such as this one, with hair styles and colors differing from the doll used as a mannequin in the catalog. *Author's collection.*

unclear, in 1951, that little toddler doll with wavable hair and sleep eyes carried on her arm a card that said, "Hi, I Am *Ginny*." The salesman's order blanks from this period did not mention this name, but listed the same old stock number and description. Orders for the new dolls came pouring in, and written across the order blank was the name "*Ginny*." The public wanted this little girl to have an identity. Still not convinced this was the way to go, Mrs. Graves issued a series of little girls with names like *Carol, Lucy, Becky, Ginger* and others. For the next

29. Here is the same doll in green, with a matching straw hat. The author has seen cases where sometime the company used a big hair bow as in the previous illustration, in place of a hat. Either are correct on some early outfits. *Ann Tardie collection.*

30. A platinum-blonde "poodle-cut" in #26, "Kindergarten Series." This hair color seems the most difficult to find today. *Ann Tardie collection.*

26

31. Transitional dolls from the "Bridal Series" in 1950. *Gidget Donnelly collection.*

32. A 1950 Transitional Sweetheart *Ginny* marked "Vogue Sweetheart Valentine #1." *Gidget Donnelly collection.*

two years, the name "*Ginny*" was just one of many of the little girl dolls produced by Vogue.

By 1952, Mrs. Graves daughter, Virginia, had a daughter of her own. Nicknamed "Pixie," she had short, curly hair that was luxuriously thick. Virginia decided that this would make a great doll wig, and developed a way to make natural lambskin into wigs, utilizing the natural curly wave pattern to her advantage.

36. *Carol*, identified in company catalogs. #26 "Kindergarten Afternoon Series." These name dolls are very collectible as they date just before the name *Ginny* was assigned. *Ann Tardie collection.*

37. A 1953 *Bridesmaid* #56, in light blue. *Thea Crozier collection.*

38. Vogue made a very few *Ginny* dolls in African-American versions. This doll is solid black plastic- not just painted on the surface. #43 "Tiny Miss Series," 1952. *Ann Tardie collection.*

39. Every collector dreams of finding a doll like *Cheryl*, #44 1953, mint-in-box like this one. Vogue was now starting to use a box with a largo. *Ann Tardie collection.*

40. The big name change! "*Ginny* Series" was the title of this little velvet outfit, #81, 1952. *Ann Tardie collection.*

45. The name "*Ginny*" keeps appearing and disappearing until 1954. This is *Becky*, #62 one of the "Debutante Series" from 1953. Tied to her arm is a little acetate box of curlers and a styling cape. *Ann Tardie collection.*

46. "Kindergarten Afternoon" produced this lovely *Kay*. (Hairstyles and colors may differ from catalogs on all strung dolls). *Ann Tardie collection.*

47. "Tiny Miss Series," #341, *June*, dressed in red and white plaid. *Ann Tardie collection*.

48. 1952 *Bridesmaid* from the "Bridal Series." *Ann Tardie collection*.

53. 1952 *Tiny Miss*, #42, in blue organdy, with daisy trimmed hat. *Thea Crozier Collection.*

54. The *Rainbow Ballerina* from 1953 is a very rare doll. Her dress is made up of different colored ribbons sewn together at top and bottom. *Thea Crozier collection.*

55. 1952 *Tyrolean Boy*. His sister is out there someplace! Like the "Brother-Sister Series," these dolls were sold individually. *Ann Tardie collection.*

56. 1951-52 unidentified dresses, not shown in catalogs. In an interview, Virginia Graves Carlson said that Vogue made many store specials over the years. Perhaps these are in that category. *Thea Crozier collection.*

61. 1952 *Tiny Miss* #43 in yellow organdy. *Thea Crozier collection*.

62. 1952 "Kindergarten Series," #21. *Ann Tardie collection*.

63. 1953 "Tiny Miss Series," *Beryl*, mint-in-box with wrist tag that says "HI,...I'm *Ginny*." *Ann Tardie collection.*

64. The "poodle-cuts" were so versatile, they could pass as boys. This is a 1952 *Wee Willie Winkie* from "Frolicking Fables Series." *Ann Tardie collection.*

65. 1952 *Pamela #60.*

70. 1953 *April*, #24, in multicolored polka dots. *Thea Crozier collection.*

71. 1953 *Cathy*, #61 Mint-green color scheme. *Thea Crozier collection.*

72. 1951 *June,* #41. "Tiny Miss Series," Cloth daisies on the hat are a nice touch. *Thea Crozier collection.*

73. 1952. *Sister* of "Brother-Sister Series." #36, in red plaid, #34 in blue stripe. *Ann Tardie collection.*

74. 1953 "Twin Series" *Cowboy*, #37, *Cowgirl*, #38. These dolls have silk-screened rodeo scenes on felt costumes. Truly representative of the "Golden Age" of dolls. *Author's collection.*

75. 1952 "Hi…I'm *Ginny*" with her "E-Z-Do Wardrobe." The red plaid accessories would be a logo for *Ginny* later on. *Author's collection.*

Now Ginny Walks

By 1954, every possible "theme" for *Ginny* had been devised and tried. "Frolicking Fables," "Square Dancer Series," "Kindergarten School Series," all gave Virginia a chance to use her vast knowledge of design and fabrics. Her ability was improving with each passing year on garments, no matter what size. Vogue, Madame Alexander, and Effanbee were all putting out products using Post-War technology. New materials such as plastics and synthetics for clothing and wigs, as well as garments, were opening new doors for the toy business.

The larger dolls of the period were going through many transitions. A new material, vinyl (polyvinylchloride), originally developed to mold bottles out of plastic instead of glass for safety reasons, was adding a new dimension to doll making. It was soon determined that the new vinyl

76. Silk-screened felt was a popular medium for Virginia Carlson. This little girl also has a "Talon" zipper in her outfit. Her dog "Sparky" is ready for a romp. Outfit #71, dog stock number is #831. *Ann Tardie collection.*

material could be soft to the touch, and resemble human skin. As technology improved, new processes were developed for inserting hair into vinyl, creating life-like head with rooted hair. This alone revolutionized the dolls of this period. Now any hairstyle was possible.

Vogue, however, did not want to change the format of *Ginny*. Bille as "Indestructible," Mrs. Graves liked the sturdy hard plastic. The big selling point of *Ginny* was her ability to go everywhere with the child. Even if the wig was destroyed through a play period such as "barber shop," it could be easily replaced for a nominal fee. There was very little that could be done to hurt *Ginny*. If you cut the hair on a vinyl doll, that is it. But *Ginny* could be given a new "coiffure" in a few minutes. Most stains wiped off the hard material.

Still, Mrs. Graves and Virginia worried that technology would outpace *Ginny*. She needed another feature that would allow her to compete with larger dolls, without sacrificing the indestructibility of the product. The answer was to make *Ginny* "walk." The big dolls of the period now had this feature in the form of one leg that automatically caught up to the other, as if taking a step, when the doll was led. Sometimes the head turned from side to side. This concept seemed perfect for a little

77. The rare African-American *Ginny* was also issued as a walker. Outfit is similar to #74, but the fabric is completely different. *Ann Tardie collection.*

78. *Party* #74. New for this series was a "Carry-All Box" that could become a clothes closet. *Author's collection.*

79. New for 1954 was the "My First Corsage Series." This is #60. The acetate box contains a small corsage. *Ann Tardie collection.*

doll like *Ginny*! Soon a mechanism was added to the doll to allow her head to turn in concert with her walk. This, of course, would mean wear and tear on her feet, so Virginia designed a pair of sturdy shoes for *Ginny* to wear, made of vinyl plastic with a little side strap and button that could easily be fastened. On the bottom of the shoes it said "*Ginny.*" This was the perfect compromise to keep *Ginny* current. Now a child could walk *Ginny* on table tops, floors, and walls. Her footwear could withstand the same punishment as the doll itself.

80. Separate coats, such as this #282, were popular in 1954.

were walkers with plastic shoes. The extra outfits, arriving in the stores later in the year, almost all included the new plastic shoes. We must keep in mind that Vogue, like other doll companies, was making toys, not collectibles, and that old stock would be used up before new stock was introduced. Today, while catalogs offer a great deal of information to the collector, it must be remembered that many variations occurred.

1954 dolls are marked "GINNY" on the black along with "VOGUE DOLLS, INC. PAT. PENDING. MADE IN U.S.A." The eyelashes are still painted,

84. 1954 beach outfit #48 with a rare *Ginny* accessory called "Freddie the Fish." He is inflatable vinyl and gaily painted. *Ann Turdie collection.*

85. 1954 "My First Corsage" walker African-American *Ginny*. #60. *Gidget Donnelly collection.*

86. *Davy Crockett.* Not shown in the catalog, Davy has many features including a "Frontier Scout" button, and a patch for the child to sew on his/her jacket. *Author's collection.*

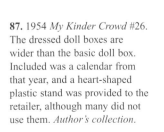

87. 1954 *My Kinder Crowd* #26. The dressed doll boxes are wider than the basic doll box. Included was a calendar from that year, and a heart-shaped plastic stand was provided to the retailer, although many did not use them. *Author's collection.*

55

92. One of the most popular outfits is this sweater and shirt set with matching hat, embroidered with the name "*Ginny*" all over the sweater. This year (1954) it came in both pink and yellow. #30 in the catalog. *Ann Tardie collection.*

Also new this year was furniture, made of fine wood and painted pink. The red plaid used for *Ginny*'s accessories would soon be her "designer" identity, and new "Series" groups, such as "Whiz Kids" and "My First Corsage Series," would help round out *Ginny*'s versatility.

All in all, 1954 was a very exciting year for *Ginny*!

93. One of the most charming sets made for *Ginny* is this "Trip Mates" luggage set. From this year on. *Ginny* had a "designer luggage signature" with her own plaid design. *Author's collection.*

1955-1956
Molded Lashes & Pretty Clothes

By 1955, *Ginny*'s identity as a household word was established. *Ginny* could be found everywhere from the finest department stores to the corner drug store. Mrs. Graves firmly believed that every child, not just the wealthy, should have access to *Ginny* dolls.

Mrs. Graves and Virginia knew that keeping *Ginny* current would insure new customers, as well as repeat customers. By having the same size doll each year, one ran the risk that customers would simply buy new clothing for their old dolls. To avoid this obvious pitfall, two things were added in 1955.

The walker mechanism was kept intact from 1954, only now the body was marked with a patent number (2687594). The new innovation of 1955 was molded eyelashes. Gone were the painted-on lashes of previous years. *Ginny* now had a rigid plastic eyelashes that made her even more durable and washable. *Ginny*'s furniture line was expanded to include a very clever gym set, which obviously had to

94. Truly a dream come true, is this doll from 1955. Mint-in-box with her catalog, she is similar to outfit #24 of that year, except her lace trim is made of heart shaped lace. On her wrist is that plastic "I Love You" heart used on earlier dolls. Her box is marked "Valentine Girl," so one can only assume she was a special for Valentine's Day that year! *Author's collection.*

have many dolls to play on it, resulting in children wanting more *Ginny* dolls. Ginnette, the little vinyl sister of *Ginny*, was added to the line. The first all-vinyl doll of the Vogue doll family, she could wear splendid clothing that were miniature versions of *Ginny*s lovely outfits. Interestingly, *Ginnette* was not in proportion to *Ginny*, but children didn't seem to mind as *Ginnette* became a huge success.

The "Series" names were dropped, and new titles such as "Bon-Bons," "Merry Moppets," and "*Ginny* Gym Kids" were added. The extra accessories offered that year were staggering. Jewelry, eyeglasses, roller and ice skates, curlers, boxed shoes and socks, note paper *Ginny* had more accessories than any doll in

99. 1955 #46. This year Mrs. Carlson redesigned the Dutch costume and made a short dress. *Thea Crozier collection.*

100. 1955 #65 formals. These lovely formals came in several colors.

history! Virginia Carlson introduced a budget line of fashions while expanding *Ginny's* fabulous wardrobe to deluxe proportions. Best of all were the fitted wardrobe chests, including dolls and clothing.

To those of us who were children in 1955, *Ginny* was a part of our lives. Stores, newspapers, and magazines were filled with either dolls themselves or mentions of them. The name "*Ginny*" was one that would not soon be forgotten.

In 1956, The *Ginny* Doll Club was started so that little children could correspond with *Ginny* and other *Ginny* doll collectors. It is obvious from reading these early letters that little boys had *Ginny* dolls as well. Let's face it...*Ginny* was exciting! Little boys found the Cowboy *Ginny* and the other dolls of the line to be as comforting as did little girls. *Ginny* was once again living up to Mrs. Graves personal crusade for liberation from stereotypes.

101. 1955 #184, extra fur coats made of real rabbit fur. These were available in pink, white, and blue. *Ann Tardie collection.*

By the end of 1956, *Ginnette* also had moving eyes, and *Ginny* had a huge cardboard doll house and dog house for "Sparky." The Vogue doll era was in full swing!

102. 1955 #62 *Ginny* had luxurious sleepwear, such as this peignoir of flocked organdy with a plain nightie. *Ann Tardie collection.*

103. 1955 #64. *Ginny* as a bride. These outfits were merely issued for fantasy play, and were never publicized the way *Ginny*'s other adventure outfits were. *Ann Tardie collection.*

104. 1955 #56. Turquoise and gold outfit with gold slippers. *Ann Tardie collection.*

105. 1955 #61. A stunning check suit for travel! *Ann Tardie collection.*

106. 1956 #6402 on the left in yellow, and #43, 1955, on the right. *Ann Tardie collection.*

106. A perfectly mint-in-box 1955 # 26 *Ginny*. Some old store stock from this period has survived and has found its way into collections. *Author's collection.*

107. 1956 *Ballerina*. #6045. The *Ginny* "Ballerina Series" has always been popular with both children and collectors. *Ann Tardie collection.*

108. 1956 *Brownie,* #6052 many little girls of 1956 belonged to the Brownies. *Ann Tardie collection.*

110. 1956 #6064. This very unusual dress is made of organdy, with slices of crayon melted into the fabric. Very desirable formal from this period. *Author's collection.*

109. 1956 *Nun*, #6065 Another "Fantasy" play outfit also sold as a separate costume. *Author's collection.*

111. 1956 *Roller Skater* and *Ice Skater* (6047-6050) Again, Virginia Carlson shows her incredible design talents in these two lovely dolls. *Ann Tardie collection.*

116. A group of late 1950s dolls in the "Hospital" *Ginny*s lent themselves to every play situation imaginable. *Author's collection.*

117. 1956 *Clown*, #6041. One of the most sought after dolls of this year, this outfit came either on a dressed doll or separately. All the dolls this author has examined have had braids, with one pink ribbon tie, and one blue ribbon tie, and leatherette tie shoes. The pompon slippers often seen on this doll are separate bedroom slippers, the same as in the "suitcase" accessory pack. *Author's collection.*

1957-1960
The End of an Era

By 1957, the name *Ginny* was known to virtually every child in America. Now the best selling doll of its kind in this country, Vogue was expanding its family.

Big sister *Jill*, a 10in (25.4cm) high-heel teen doll, was a new introduction. *Jill* was truly an innovation and years before her time. Her face was *Ginny's* face, slightly grown up, with the same rosy cheeks and sleep-eyes used for *Ginny* dolls. Her hair was in a ponytail or flip style and, like *Ginny*, replacement wigs were available. She had bending knees, and gorgeous clothes, most of which were "big sister" versions of *Ginny's* lovely clothing. Virginia Carlson dressed *Jill* in the real life fashions of the period. America was having a love affair with high fashion! Mrs. Graves, still con-cerned that the public would out-grow *Ginny*, felt *Jill* would be the perfect answer to playing in the future as well as the present. For

118. 1957 #7091, *Communion*. Another of the outfits highlighting special events in a little girl's life is this lovely lacy commu-nion dress. The locket says "*Ginny*: on it and is very rare accessory. *Author's collection.*

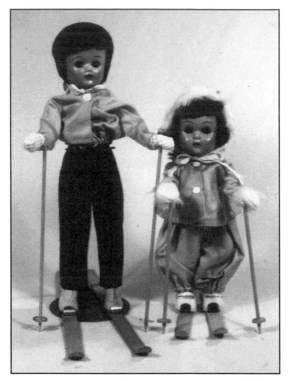

several years, *Jill* dominated the teen-doll market.

Mrs. Graves always tried to keep *Ginny* current. A new feature, bending knees, gave *Ginny* even more play value, and like the features that came before, it was done in a way that would not make the doll more fragile, just more versatile, Virginia Carlson designed over 60 new outfits for *Ginny* in that year alone. Formal gowns, long a staple of the 1955-56 lines, were carried over and redesigned with styling details even real garments lacked. Collectors refer to the 1957 formal gowns as some of the best of all the Vogue doll clothing.

Other new ideas in 1957 included a "Party Package" which highlighted *Ginny* and extra clothes, and an apron set for *Ginny* and her little mother. Also new that year were "Knit Kits," so a child could hand knit clothes for *Ginny*.

In 1958, The Vogue doll family included *Jill* and her girl-

124. *Ginny* and *Jill* go skiing! These matching outfits exemplify the wide range of matching costumes available for *Jill* and *Ginny*.

125. The "*Ginny* Gym Set," surrounded by various years' *Ginny*s, and *Jill*s. The play value of a set like this is extraordinary! *Author's collection.*

126. 1957 #7060. The cover outfit for the 1957 catalog. This pink velveteen costume came in a matching version for *Jill* and *Ginnette*. *Author's collection.*

127. 1957 #7865. This untouched old stock gift set complete with cardboard overliner, is a collectors treasure! The "Fitted Vacation Trunk" includes a doll in basic panties, dressed in nightie and robe in waffle piqué and a cowgirl outfit, a houndstooth check school dress, raincoat, hat and a formal. Its original price is $15! *Ann Tardie collection.*

128. 1957 #7866. "Fitted Trousseau Chest." This gorgeous pink wooden box features trays that swing out and include *Ginny* in a bride outfit, five additional outfits, fur coat, raincoat, umbrella, and many accessories. It's original price was $29.95. The box could be used for a jewelry box late on. It is almost impossible to even place a value today on such a find! *Ann Tardie collection.*

134. 1959 #1259, *Hawaiian*. This fabulous outfit would later be copied by other companies, but the wonderful wooden surf board would belong only to *Ginny! Ann Tardie collection*

135. 1960 #9131 *Wee Imp*. This friend of *Ginny*s had straight red hair, green eyes, and freckles. She was referred to as "Mischievous."(*Note:* The Wee Imp had four outfits all her own, but are tagged the same as *Ginny*s.) *Ann Tardie collection.*friend of *Ginny*s had straight red hair, green eyes, and freckles. She was referred to as "Mischievous."(*Note:* The *Wee Imp* had four outfits all her own, but are tagged the same as *Ginny*s.) *Ann Tardie collection.*

The 1960s - And Ginny !

By the 1960s, Saturday morning television had become a big event in the life of a child. Allegedly Mrs. Graves did not believe in television advertising. By 1961, virtually every household in America either had a television set or had access to one through relatives and friends.

Mrs. Graves felt that choosing a suitable toy was the parent's responsibility. *Ginny*, in fact, had been endorsed by *Parents* magazine!

Attention to teenage sophistication by other fashion dolls really took a toll on the image of *Ginny*. In 1961, *Jeff*, *Jan* and the hard plastic *Jill* were discontinued. In 1962, *Ginny* had only 15 new outfits. In 1963, a vinyl head with rooted hair was added to *Ginny*. She was marked on the back "*GINNY* VOGUE DOLLS, INC. PAT NO. 2687594, Made in U.S.A.." The doll had 15 outfits designed for her. 1964 saw only 13 new outfits. *Ginny* was slowly being phased out. Vogue had gone

136. In the early 1960s *Ginny*'s head became vinyl. The body was the walker body from 1957. *Ann Tardie collection.*

142. 1966 # 102 *Mary Lamb*. These "Made in USA" styles had a charm all their own. *Ann Tardie collection.*

143. The 1969 #522 *Bride* is as pretty as any *Ginny* ever made. This dress is made of the finest heavy slipper satin. The flower cascade is original. (Original Price is $7 on her tag!) *Author's collection.*

into the manufacturing of baby dolls, and was having a moderate success. The company had found a new direction.

1965 saw *Ginny* as an all-vinyl doll marked "*Ginny*" on her head, and "*GINNY* VOGUE DOLLS, INC." on her back. She came dressed in a few little girl costumes, five "Fairytale Land," and nine "Far-Away Lands" styles. This all-vinyl *Ginny* has withstood the test of time, and is a lovely little doll. Interestingly, 19 years later, the new Vogue *Ginny*s would be the doll a new generation of mothers would remember. Collectors are discovering more and more the desirability of the "Made in USA" vinyl *Ginny* dolls. Also in 1965, a series of vinyl *Jill* dolls were introduced as a special "History Land Series."

By 1966, the "Made in U.S.A." vinyl *Ginny* had attracted some attention and the line was expanded. Some old series were rejuvenated, such as "Fairytale Land" and "Far-Away Lands," to include some gorgeous pairs of dolls, and a *Ginny* Nun was again available. Even the "regular" costumes for *Ginny* included some party dresses and play clothes that were fresh and imaginative.

By 1968, (a period often overlooked by collectors), *Ginny* had nine regular costumes and 24 from the "Far-Away Lands Series," and special dolls such as the *Nun, Nurse, Bride, Cowgirl, Pilgrim,* and *Stewardess* constitute some of the rarest dolls of that period by Vogue.

1969 was the last year of the American-made *Ginny*s. She had ten costumes for everyday, and 12 in the "Far-Away Lands Series."

144. Many experiments were tried in the 1960s. This gorgeous 18in (46cm) *Indian* is unmarked. Her clothes are labeled, however, and she is a copy of the little Indian girl from circa 1965. The larger doll's wrist tag says. "Miss *Ginny*." No mention of this doll is in the catalog and she is most unusual. *Author's collection*.

As late as the mid 1970s it was possible to buy up old stock *Ginnys* from the 1960s. and because of the large number produced, it seemed that *Ginny* never left the marketplace.

145. Shown with a 1959 *Eskimo* for comparison, this 12in (30.5cm). *Miss Ginny* is also dressed for the North. Her face is identical to the larger *Miss Ginny*. She is marked "Vogue" on her head: clothing is labeled. *Author's collection.*

146. A group of all-vinyl "Made in USA" *Ginny* dolls. *Author's collection.*

The 1970s
The Story Continues!

By the 1970s, the Graves family and Virginia Carlson were no longer were involved with Vogue. Mrs. Carlson had retired to tend to her mother, and Joan Cornette was now chief designer. By 1972 *Ginny* was manufactured in Hong Kong, using the same mold for the vinyl "USA" doll. She was marked "*GINNY*" on the back of her head and "VOGUE DOLLS (1972 Made in Hong Kong" on the back. A few interesting Hong Kong *Ginny*s are collectible, such as the African doll and a "Gift Set" containing a doll and extra clothing.

In 1973, Vogue, always a family owned business, was sold to the Tonka Corporation. Interested in the name "Vogue" because of its meaning in the doll world. The company continued the Melrose, Massachusetts plant. By 1975 *Ginny* was not the mainstay of the company. Dolls such as *Miss Ginny*, 15in (38cm) dressed in "mod" clothing, were in the new chain toy stores. By 1976, the "Far-Away Lands Series" was the only style available. Dolls dressed in "little girl" clothing had been discontinued.

147. 1972 #1802, *Africa*. Considered by most collectors to be a valuable doll of the Hong Kong period. *Ann Tardie collection.*

148. 1977 *Jamaican* and *Colonial Girl.*
Made in Hong Kong, but with painted eyes.
These are highly collectible as they were
made for only one year. *Ann Tardie
Collection.*

In 1977, Vogue Dolls Inc. became a subsidiary of Lesney Products, and moved the entire operation to Moonachie, New Jersey. Lesney, continued the "Far-Away Lands" dolls, and used a new mold for another series with painted eyes that included an American Pioneer Girl. This doll is lovely, and was a refreshing new change in *Ginny*'s history.

The biggest surprise to collectors, however, came at Toy Fair in 1978. Lesney had decided to rejuvenate *Ginny*. At Toy Fair in New York a media blitz announced in proud headlines that *"Ginny* is Back!." The advertising was definitely aimed at the mother of the little girl who once owned *Ginny* herself. The company wanted this new generation of children to love and cherish the same doll as their mother did. Ads showed 1950s children holding *Ginny* dolls, while a new generation of children was shown with the new *Ginny!*

By 1980-1981, these dolls were given an "upbeat" image by involving a design house, Sasson, in the creation of *Ginny* fashions. The Sasson fashions were very imaginative, and capitalized on the "Roller Disco" craze, and other trends of the time.

Soon, however, America, children, and collectors were ready for a new *Ginny* by 1984!

149. *Good Housekeeping* ad, 1979.
Lesney's campaign was aimed at mothers
who loved *Ginny* themselves. *Ann Tardie
collection.*

150. 1972 #1001 "Gift Set." This set is a great collectible of the Hong Kong period. The box says "Vogue Dolls, Melrose, MA 02176. A subsidiary of Tonka Corporation." *Ann Tardie collection.*

151. A valuable Lesney *Ginny* is this *Ginnette*. She is the black version of *Ginny*. It is interesting that the old name was used for this doll! The reason remains a mystery! *Author's collection.*

153. This poster was included in "*Ginny's* Sweet Shoppe," a play setting for 1979. *Ann Tardie collection.*

152. The Lesney furniture was very imaginative and had lots of great accessories. *Ann Tardie collection.*

154. The moped made by Lesney is the hardest to find of the 1978-1979 accessories. *Ann Tardie collection.*

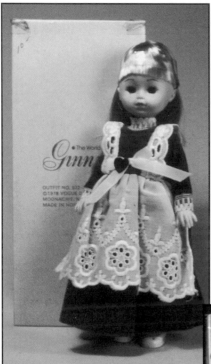

155. Catalog houses such as Sears, Penneys, and Montgomery Wards carried the Lesney *Ginny*s. They were shipped in plain white boxes such as this. *Author's collection.*

156. The real "prize" of the Lesney period will be the "Special Gift Pack." Sealed in plastic, most will not survive intact. These were listed in the catalog, but not widely available. *Author's collection.*

157. Lesney *Ginny*s enjoying an evening at home! *Ann Tardie collection.*

158. "*Ginny*'s Sweet Shoppe" from 1979, with a juke box and popcorn machine. *Ann Tardie collection.*

159. The name "Sasson" gave the Lesney *Ginny*s an upbeat image! *Author's collection.*

1984 - 1985
A New Beginning

In 1983, Lesney's last attempt at *Ginny* dolls was a series of "International Brides." The Oriental dolls were especially nice, and the series is necessary to a comprehensive *Ginny* collection. Later that year, Lesney ceased to exist as a toy company.

In October 1983, Walter (Wally) Reiling, a man with 30 years of experience in the toy business, secured the rights to both *"Ginny"* and "Vogue." As president of Meritus Industries, a New Jersey based company, Mr. Reiling was in many ways like Jennie Graves. A forward thinking man, Wally viewed *Ginny* the same way Mrs. Graves did. In 1984, at Toy Fair in New York, Vogue dolls again opened its doors. The new dolls, delightful in every way, recaptured the *Ginny* of the late

160. Vogue made this exclusive *Ginny Fairy Godmother* in 1986 just for Meyers a store in northern New Jersey that carried *Ginny* right from the beginning. *Ann Tardie collection.*

1960s, and even held their own with the gorgeous strung dolls of the 1950s. Mr. Reiling displayed the new *Ginny* next to a beautiful mint doll from 1952.

New to the 1984 Vogue line were porcelain *Ginny* dolls, making this the first time *Ginny* had been offered in porcelain. The line included many different hair styles

and colors, just like the *Ginny* of old!

In 1985, Vogue, under Mr. Reiling's guidance, introduced *Ginnette*, the baby sister of *Ginny*. Also available in porcelain, she is made much the same way *Ginnette* was constructed in the 1950s. Pairs such as Bride and Groom, Hansel and Gretel and Jack and *Jill* bring back fond memories.

The reissue of the *Coronation Queen*. The most luxurious doll of the Golden Era of the 1950s. Once again made *Ginny* queen of the 1980s.

161. 1984 *Antique Lace* in red, and *Holiday Girl* in blue. The beautiful fabrics and rich colors made the 1984 dolls a huge success. They were one of the few dolls able to satisfy both collector and child that year. *Ann Tardie collection.*

162. Vogue announced the return of *Ginny* done in the style of the past at Toy Fair, 1984. Children and collectors alike were delighted with the little doll. *Author's collection.*

166. *Hula Ginny*, one of my favorite dolls. The skin tones are very subtle and the entire doll is charming. *Ann Tardie collection*.

Meyers, a toy store in New Brunswick, New Jersey, had store specials produced for them by Meritus that were very successful, as did Shirley's Dollhouse in Wheeling, Illinois. The owner, Shirley Bertrand, designed the first black *Ginny* produced in hard plastic since the mid-1950s! It was so well received that other store specials were done for Shirley's Dollhouse, and without exception, they are some of the finest dolls ever produced by Dakin.

Gradually, the doll became so well known that, beginning with Toy Fair 1988, Dakin decided that *Ginny* should have a separate catalog and order form instead of being featured in their general gift catalog. Dakin retained ownership of the *Ginny* Doll Trademark until June of 1995.

Over the years, an incredible amount of work has gone into producing the most creative accessories such as furniture, jewelry, hats, purses, and shoes which could all be purchased separately.

170. *Ginny In Camelot* is the perfect fairy tale princess. The doll is shown in the 1989 catalog. *Ann Tardie collection.*

Ginny - The New Generation

In 1995 *Ginny* found a new home in Oakdale, California. At a Walt Disney World convention that year, Linda Smith (who has long been involved in the doll and toy business) was chatting with colleagues outside of the ballroom during the final banquet. She heard that *Ginny* was to be sold by Dakin. Wendy Lawton, her partner in the Lawton Doll Company, could tell Linda was excited when she came back into the room. She asked Wendy, "What doll company have we always wished we could help develop?"

That began a seven-month ordeal to acquire *Ginny*. At first, according to Lawton "We didn't think we could possibly afford to buy *Ginny*. We had marathon meetings, working the figures backward and forward between Linda nad Jim Smith, and Keith (Lawton) and me. When Linda and Jim's children, David and Susanne, heard about the opportu-

168. The *Ginny* Club Doll, *America's Sweetheart*, from the new Vogue Doll Company in 1996. For more information on the Ginny Doll Club see page 158.

All photographs in this chapter are courtesy of The Vogue Doll Company.

169. The 1997 Vogue catalog showed the "*Ginny* Travels Collection" and the Travel Doll with a navy velveteen coat.

170. *Puttin' on the Ritz*, also from the "On Stage Collection."

nity, they were just as excited. They decided to put their resources in the pot."

Jim Smith took over the negotiations. "It took more than half a year of seven-day-weeks for him to complete the purchase" Wendy reports. "We were lucky enough to have obtained a good faith agreement immediately, so that while we negotiated the deal, Dakin couldn't entertain other offers. As soon as the word had gone out that Dakin was selling, everyone was interested. Had it not been for Linda ferreting out the information before it was common knowledge, we could never have been in the running." When the purchase was complete, the

171. The *Bride and Groom* set from 1997.

Smiths and Lawtons set about all of the legal work to register all of the trademarks and solidify all of the various *Ginny* assets back under the Vogue Doll Company umbrella.

The new owners of the Vogue Doll Company are Jim and Linda Smith, Keith and Wendy Lawton, Susanne Smith and David Smith. Linda Smith is President of Vogue. She oversees the entire operation and directs each department, handles licensing and industry alliances, coordinates trade show efforts, and often travels on behalf of *Ginny*. Jim Smith,

> *The Smith/Lawton team looked carefully at the Ginny doll and immediately made some changes.*

172. The *Maid of Honor* goes well with the happy couple in photograph 171.

173. *Concert Pianist* from the "On Stage Collection".

as CFO, is director of Vogue's general administration and fulfillment, is responsible for all financial and legal aspects of the company, and oversees the ordering and import process. Wendy Lawton is the head designer. She develops the concepts, designs each *Ginny* and directs the design of the *Ginny* accessories. Linda and Jim's daughter Susanne Smith is the director of sales and marketing. She coordinates the sales representatives who offer *Ginny* to the retailers, personally works with the multi-store accounts, works with the designer and ad agency to develop the advertising and catalog, acts as director of the

176. Another flower garden theme for *Ginny* is Petunias.

fabric than the rolled hems. The shoes on the walker *Ginny* were changed from the plastic versions back to the traditional leatherette shoes with the colorful center-snap, with *Ginny*'s initial on the snap.

The new owners also made a commitment to provide better customer service. A special *Ginny*

Club service center was set up with an 800 number and a customer service staff to answer all club questions and concerns. A separate customer service department was set up for retailers, staffed with knowledgeable representatives with a serious commitment to service and customer satisfaction.

177. *Geraniums*, like the other gardening dolls, has pretend seed packets, a spade, and a flowerpot.

180. *Ginny* is fabulous in fur in her *Fifth Avenue* ensemble.

181. *Country Fair Ginny* wears two colors of gingham.

182. *Farmer's Market Ginny* wears a dress trimmed with embroidered watermelon seeds!

183. *Ginny* can also barbecue – she shares her Barbecue Burgers recipe.

184. *Caramel Apples* is another of *Ginny*'s favorite treats!

185. *Gingerbread Cookies* is one of the dolls in the "*Ginny* Cooks Collection".

facturer. They also were impressed with the professional and experienced employees. The facility was beautiful, with dormitories and recreational areas (much like a college campus) for the unmarried workers, who came from neighboring villages to work in the big city. The Smiths sat down with the owner and showed him *Ginny*, explained her history, and shared their goals and plans for her. The owner, who liked the fact that they were a family-owned business and that they cared so much about the product, later complimented them "I am impressed by the way you do business. You are a family. You are like a Chinese company."

The success at placing *Ginny* in one of the finest toy making facilities in the world still left the Smith/Lawton

186. *Ginny* loves *Hot Cocoa* at bedtime.

team with challenges to solve. Their experience with the Lawton Doll Company was in making porcelain dolls in a hands-on operation. Keeping those same high standards for *Ginny*'s manufacture was a totally different situation.

The first major problem was

110

scaling back the proportions of *Ginny's* hair. Because her construction is unique, this was more difficult than expected. *Ginny* is made of injection molded hard plastic, an expensive medium for a doll. The molds alone cost ten times more than the molds used to make vinyl dolls, plus the process is more complex and time-consuming. The new company is committed to hard plastic, however, because it is such a lasting, impervious material. Dakin created an innovation that had not been used since the tiny hard plastic *Betsy McCall* of the 1960s – they used a vinyl pate and attached it to the hard plastic head, so that this hard plastic doll could have rooted hair that could be styled. While this is more versatile than a glued-on wig, it is a very complex construction. When the new owners attempted to cut back the amount of hair, some of the first dolls shipped had hair that was too skimpy to cover the join of the hard plastic to vinyl. Most of the dolls had to be shipped back, which set the com-

187. Collectors can bake *Ginny's* French bread since the *Bakes Bread* doll comes with a recipe card.

111

188. 1997 marked the 75th Anniversary of Vogue Dolls. The "Debut Collection" brought back classics such as *Walk in the Park* and *Day at the Beach*.

189. Also from the "Debut Collection" is the classic *Happy Birthday*.

pany back months. It took much trial and error to find the most pleasing proportions for the hair.

A *Ginny* doll may require as long as eight months to be made from start to finish. Director of Design Wendy Lawton explains the process. "The concept comes first… the idea for the doll and for the series. Since *Ginny* has a long-standing personality, I try to determine what *Ginny* would like to do,

190. *First Ballet* brings back the *Ginny* ballerina with her crisp organdy tutu.

191. Music Recital and *Sunday Best* are two dolls from the 1997 "Debut Collection."

192. *School Days Ginny* proudly wears her pleated skirt and monogrammed sweater.

would like to wear... and then I look at fabrics and colors for costuming." Next she sketches the doll and tries out several colors or looks. The fabric choice is made with close attention to the scale and weight of the material. Then samples are made. "It usually takes four or five samples to get the costume just right. My sample maker generally does all the machine work, while I do the

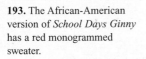

193. The African-American version of *School Days Ginny* has a red monogrammed sweater.

194. *Dress Me Blonde* and *Dress Me Brunette* are waiting for new wardrobes.

hand-sewing and trimming." Then the hair color, hairstyle, painting style and eye color are chosen. "Finally I choose shoes, hats, accessories – everything that goes with that particular *Ginny*. Many times the accessories are hand sculpted or the models are created out of wood." When a perfect sample doll is ready "we take photographs and do precise specification sheets, noting the tiniest

195. The "Dress Me Collection" consists of dolls that come in organdy teddies ready for the collector to choose a new dress pack. These are the African-American and red haired versions.

196. *Ginny's Trunk* is the perfect accessory to keep her extra clothes in great shape.

detail. The patterns are copied and swatches of the fabric are attached to a reference card. The hairstyle is drawn in detail." David Smith then familiarizes himself with every aspect of the design before sending the complete package to the factory for initial sampling.

Fortunately for the new owners of Vogue, retailers and collectors were quick to welcome them. As Linda Smith expressed it "The retailers who carried *Ginny* in their stores were delighted since Dakin had been having a difficult time and had not produced any new product nor fulfilled club obligations for between one and two years." The new company has gone from a nonexistent dealer base to more than 1000 retailers and now has over 80 items in the line.

As the new team points out: "Collectors never stopped buying *Ginny*. There continues to be a dynamic collecting community for *Ginny* – in clubs, in conventions, online and through dealers… we are still amazed at the power of this eight-inch personality."

197. Only *Ginny* would have a special smock dress for Art Class.

initial 'G
(my moth
to know t
of *Ginny*
Dakin ret
Ginny D
June of 1

Over
ble amou
into prod
accessori
jewelry, b
which co
separately

198. *Party Pretty* and *Sail Away* are two clothing packs for the "Dress Me" *Ginny*s.

199. *Pink Parfait* is another ensemble which is sold separately.

204. Two more "Dress Me" clothing packs are *Spring Bouquet* and *Sleepy Time*.

205. *Denim* and *Chambray* is an outfit practical enough for *Ginny's* most demanding activities.

122

206. *Hearts and Flowers* would make a lovely Valentine's Day outfit for *Ginny*.

207. The *Ginny* Doll Club Doll for 1997, celebrating the 75th Anniversary of the Vogue Doll Company, is the *Diamond Jubilee Princess*. For more information on the Ginny Doll Club see page 158.

208. *Pretty in Plaid* is the 1998 Club Doll.

209. *Ginny Photographs Yosemite* is part of the "*Ginny Travels Collection*".

210. *Ginny Hits The Big Apple* and is prepared to shop!

211. The *Trapeze Artist* is a star in the little circus.

212. *Ring Master* heads "*Ginny*'s Little Circus Collection" for 1998.

213. *Ginny* may be the most colorful *Clown* ever!

214. *Tightrope Walker* holds a parasol to help her balance on the high wire.

215. *Bareback Rider* is an event exclusive for 1998.

216. *Ice Skates* is one of the dolls in the "Fabulous Fifties Collection", new in 1998.

217. The record on *Ginny*'s circular skirt brings back memories of the 50s.

218. This cute *Car Hop* roller skates those burgers to hungry customers.

219. *Prom Night Ginny* is ready to dance in her pale pink gown.

220. *Ice Cream Parlor* brings back nostalgic memories of special treats.

221. *Dance of the Sugarplum Fairy* is a 1998 addition to the "On Stage Collection."

222. The "*Ginny* Celebrates Collection" has a *First Communion* doll in blonde.

223. This is the brunette version of *First Communion.*

224. *First Communion* also comes as a Hispanic doll.

225. *Sweet Pea* is a 1998 addition to the "*Ginny* Gardens Collection."

226. *Kindergarten Cute* is a 1998 addition to the "School Days Collection."

227. This is the African-American version of *Sweet Pea*.

228. *Ginny Bunny* is reminiscent of the now rare *Ginny Easter Bunnies* of the 1950s.

229. *Bobby Soxer*, in the teens' "uniform" of the 50s, wears jeans, a letter sweater, and has a perky pony tail.

230. A new doll in 1998 to the *"Ginny Cooks Collection"* is *Banana Split*.

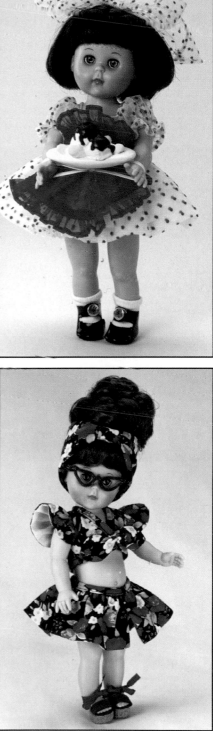

231. *Pajama Party* has *Ginny* ready to phone her best pals.

232. *Cabana Casual* is a colorful addition to the "Fabulous Fifties Collection."

A. The *Ginny* Accessories

No doll in the 1950s had as many accessories as did *Ginny*. Everything from earmuffs to schoolbags was available for this little toddler doll. Stores carried racks of items, such as extra shoes, socks and eyeglasses. Separates, such as skirts, slacks and hats, were also sold. *Ginny* even had her very own printed sheets long before designer linen was in "vogue".

To many collectors the accessories are the fun part! Here is a sampling of some accessories available for *Ginny*!

233. *Ginny* Apron set #7837. This was a cute set for "Mother and *Ginny*." *Ann Tardie collection.*

234. 1958 *Ginny* separates. *Ann Tardie collection.*

235. Assorted jewelry. Top is 1956 #6834, a pearl ensemble. Beneath is a charm bracelet, 1958 #3690, with heads of *Jill*, *Ginny*, and *Ginnette* in silver. ($2.00 from Filene's in Boston!) Bottom is *Ginnys* locket, 1955 #835. *Ann Tardie collection.*

236. MIB *Ginny* stands marked Vogue Dolls, 1952-53 and Vogue Dolls, Inc., 1954. *Gidget Donnelly collection.*

137

237. A 1953 Beach *Ginny* with a rare
"Freddie the Fish" and store display sign.
Gidget Donnelly collection.

238. Various years mint in box clothing to
show the boxes. *Author's collection.*

239. More of the gorgeous accessories available for *Ginny* during the Golden Era! *Author's collection.*

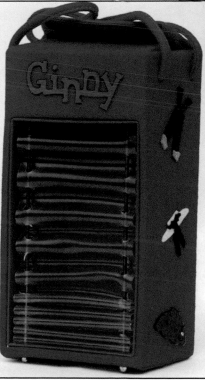

240. More of the gorgeous accessories including note paper which came in a gift set with doll called "Party package"...the red plaid itels used a plaid that was *Ginny's* "signature."

241. #7863 is a Gadabout Case from 1957. The name can be in various colors. *Gidget Donnelly collection.*

242. Everything could be purchased for *Ginny* separately in the heyday of the 1950s! *Ann Tardie collection.*

243. #1580 is a Christmas Stocking from 1958. *Gidget Donnelly collection.*

B. Why Collect *Ginny* Dolls?

Originally conceived and manufactured as a child's toy, *Ginny* took on a personality all her own right from the start. In the 1950s, considered by many to be the "Golden Years" of doll collecting, *Ginny* went unrecognized as the symbol of liberation for an entire generation of women. It is only today, with our educated hindsight, that we see this doll for the brilliant statement that she makes.

In *Ginny's* wardrobe, the same factors prevail, *Ginny* has outfits to be a cowgirl, an ice skater, a skier, a chef, and has a tailored wardrobe to indulge in riding, surfing, and tennis. What made this interesting is that through *Ginny* a child was not playing in the future as with high-heel teen dolls, but was playing right now

... in the present. With *Ginny*, a child could achieve the courage and the savoir-faire to go out and do, not just dream of a distant time when this might happen.

Interestingly, little boys are attracted to *Ginny* dolls, too. Vogue *Ginny* Doll Fan Club Newsletters are full of letters from little boys who regard *Ginny* as the same personal friend that little girls do. Why this cross over of traditional roles? Because *Ginny* and her adventures are exciting, and this excitement knows no gender. *Ginny* is designed to have fun with. Her very construction allows her to be taken every place from the dirt hill to the swimming hole; from the roller rink to the ski slopes. Today, with our understanding of human nature, it is easy to sit back and say that Mrs. Graves put much of her own personality into *Ginny*. Perhaps even she was not aware that so much of herself and her own struggles were being revealed in the doll. But to children the message was clear. If *Ginny* can do it and not be afraid so can I.

The proverbial "boogie man" was put to rest when *Ginny* took that first step. A train trip, a day at Grandma's a barbecue, all seem like nothing to adults, but to a child, these precious firsts are a challenge. *Ginny* dolls taught a child to take those first precious steps, and stand tall and proud. The little owner of *Ginny* could see that this little girl, 1/8th her size, could do it, and so could she. Add that to the virtually indestructible composition of the doll itself, and you can see that fears were laid to rest. Send *Ginny* up in a basket in a tree…she will make it back down. Take her swimming…she won't melt. All this added greatly to the self-confidence of a child.

Today, we as adults, reared in the heyday of *Ginny*, view her as a source of strength for our attitudes. One cannot underestimate the value and the lasting impact a doll like *Ginny* has on the life of a child.

C. How To Collect *Ginny* Dolls

In dolls, we really only have two classifications. A doll is either perfect…perhaps old store stock, or bought for an older child and stashed away in a closet for twenty years, or it is an orphan, in need of a new wig, and lots of tender loving care. My advice is really simple…enjoy both types of dolls and love them both, only understand the difference.

Collecting dolls is perhaps one of the most rewarding of all hobbies, but like with all interests, the collector should buy with an understanding of the market. With *Ginny* dolls, one should avoid the so-called "middle market" dolls that are played with but original and commanding almost mint prices. These dolls are for the person who does not know what a mint doll is, and settles for less, paying a premium price for imperfection. It is almost impossible to recoup your investment in a doll such as this. You would be smarter to do one of two things, either buy a nude, played with doll and restore it yourself with original clothes, or pay a premium price for a premium doll. Both methods will net you a great doll of value, and one that will surely bring you happiness!

Standards vary for collecting *Ginny* dolls from different years. The early bisque "Just Me" dolls and the composition dolls can be forgiven the sins of neglect…of wigs not tended to or of clothes improperly bleached. But the newer the doll, the more perfect it should be in order to bring the figure listed in price guides. Collecting played with dolls if the price is right can also be rewarding, as long as the seller and the buyer realize that it is being purchased for pleasure, and not as a fine collectible.

Fortunately, *Ginny* dolls are one of the sturdiest dolls ever made. The restoration of a *Ginny* doll (discussed in a later segment of this book) is a fairly simple thing to do. *Ginny* can be made whole again, without much professional guidance.

Certain models of *Ginny* are more expensive than others. The strung dolls of the early 1950s, before *Ginny* really had her identity, seem to be the most collectible at this writing, and with good reason. They are artistically and esthetically perfect. With their Nutex Wigs, and delicate sleep eyes, they are real treasures of the Vogue Doll Company. The next in desirability are the painted eye hard plastics manufactured between 1948 and 1950, followed by the molded lash walkers of the 1955 period. Today's collector of *Ginny* is sophisticated, and eager to acquire new acquisitions. We have an obligation to future generations, to preserve our doll collections. It is to this future that *Ginny* belongs.

D. The Care (and repair!) of *Ginny*

The collectors of the new *Ginny* dolls tend to be better informed than those in the past about how to protect dolls to keep them as pristine as possible. For collectors who have older dolls, particularly since *Ginny* is a play doll as well as a collectible, sometimes decisions must be made about improving the condition of a doll.

Very few dolls were made as sturdy as the composition and hard plastic *Ginny* dolls. Designed to take years of hard play, these great dolls can easily be put back to their former selves with just a little care and common sense. As discussed in a previous chapter, a nude, played with doll is basically just a mannequin, and should be priced accordingly. However, if you see a little waif, with disheveled hair, and dirty face, it can easily be made almost mint.

COMPOSITION DOLLS

Only recently have methods been devised to repair composition dolls short of repainting, which is a mistake, It is often easy to make these dolls from the 1930s and 1940s look better. Begin by restringing the doll properly. Doll supply companies sell rubber bands that are especially made for 8in (30.3cm) dolls and are very inexpensive. Using a stringing hook, start with the head, then pull the band through the body, hooking each leg onto the band. Finally, hook on each arm, making a loop inside the doll. These bands are better to use than elastic because the tension is already pre-set for this size doll. If metal hooks, usually embedded in the composition are missing, these can be replaced again from a good doll supply company. Usually a hook has just pulled out of its hole, and a new hook can be bonded with a strong metal glue into the original hole. Once the doll is restrung, she will begin to take on her former identity!

To clean a composition doll, it is important to avoid any cleaner that is water based. Nick Hill has tested all types of cleaners on dolls and recommends using either "Permatex", which is a hand cleaner sold at auto supply stores, or "Wright's Silver Polish Cream" on composition. These products will clean the composition without harming the surface. Of the two, the "Permatex" is the most heavy- duty, but it is also messy to use. Always work carefully around facial features, using a cotton swab. It may be necessary, to "touch-up" a missing eyeball, or whatever. Use a very fine brush and acrylic paints, experiment on paper first before working on the doll. Usually just a touch of black in the eye will restore the "look" that may have peeled off. If splits in the composition are visible, fill them in with some plastic wood that you have tinted with acrylics, and learn to live with the doll's imperfections, rather than allowing someone ruin the total historical value by performing a complete paint job.

The mohair wigs can be tricky, but here are a few "secrets" that may be helpful. Try to avoid washing the wig. These wigs are very delicate. The best thing is to sprinkle a little cornstarch in the wig, and using a dry toothbrush, brush it through the wig. You will be amazed at the results! To restore the curl, purchase a small curling iron sold in dime stores that is made to do "tendrils" on people. This plug-in iron with a diameter of a pencil is invaluable for human and mohair wigs. Never use it on synthetics, as it will melt the hair. Use the pencil-like iron to shape tiny curls and bangs, using a photo of a mint doll for guidance. You will be thrilled with the results.

The clothing on dolls from the 1930s and 1940s was usually made of all natural fibers such as cotton, and can be safely cleaned. Many methods have been tested. The new product "Perk" from Twin Pines of Maine is excellent. An older remedy is to fill a flat dish with lukewarm water, add about fi cup of a non-chlorine bleach ("Snowy", etc.), and let the dress soak for about 15 minutes or so. Remove, and let dry naturally. Never put a delicate dress like this in the dryer. As the dress air-dries, it can be shaped, and by the time it is dry, will not need much ironing. If ironing is needed, use a cool iron, on the wrong side of the dress, and avoid at all costs that shiny "ironed" look. Shoes can be wiped down with "Fantastic", and socks can be soaked in a no-chlorine prewash. If all this scares you, buy some ruined doll clothes at a doll show and use them to experiment on until you get the feel of working with fabrics from this period. Take your time is the most important advice.

Never begin to restore a doll right after you buy it. Live with the doll for a few days until the "newness" of your purchase wears off and you can see what you can live with in the way of damage. It is always better to do too little than too much! Nothing is sadder than a composition doll repainted, rewigged, and redressed in polyester and lace! If a new wig is needed for a composition *Ginny*, buy and old mohair wig and cut it up to make a new wig. Usually just the crown will be all that is needed. If you sew and want to copy an old dress, buy an old hankie or curtain from the period to use for your material. Never use new fabrics on an old doll.

HARD PLASTIC *GINNYS*

These dolls are much easier to restore than the composition ones. The only problems encountered are "green eyebrows" on the strung dolls. This is a natural occurrence when these dolls are exposed to strong sunlight (Beware, it can happen to MIB dolls if exposed!) An advanced collector will not accept this flaw on a mint doll, and the doll should be priced accordingly if this has occurred.

The painted-eye hard plastics and the early sleep-eye non-walkers can be strung with the same looped band as the composition dolls, following the directions given earlier.

Wigs on the sleep-eye dolls are usually saran or "Nutex," a nylon base fiber. Both can be washed right on the doll, squeezing out excess water and applying a small bit of fabric softener as a "conditioner." Leave the doll face down for a few minutes to drain the water out of the eyes. A dry toothbrush works wonders to remove grime in the eyes, and untangle the hair. The hair can be set in *Ginny's* famous "flip" by using three small rollers. One roller on each side of her face, and one in the back, rolled up, and she is herself again. Put a strip of hairset tape around her head to hold her bangs down and shape the hair to the head.

The clothing from this period is usually cotton and can be laundered as described above - but watch out for taffeta! This shiny fabric cannot be washed successfully without losing sizing, which gives it the body it needs to hold its shape. Also, it cannot be ironed without leaving shiny marks.

Shoes made of plastic can be scrubbed with cleanser and a toothbrush. Socks can be soaked in "Perk" or a non-chlorine bleach. Commercial products are also available specifically to clean dolls and doll clothing. If *Ginny* seems a bit pale, a little cream rouge on the end of your finger will restore her to perfection.

VINYL *GINNYS*

The dolls of the 1960s to the present can be cleaned with "Fantastic", and their rooted hair washed and set. As their clothes are made usually of today's miracle fibers, they can be soaked and dried and usually don't even look laundered. Don't, however, put them in the washer or dryer. The agitation is too much for a tiny garment.

Some collectors prefer to buy dolls that are in need of "love" because they enjoy bringing a doll in sad condition back to how they looked originally. Many practiced restorers have spectacular collections they have paid nothing for because they have the patience to remove the sins of neglect. Others want only untouched dolls and are willing to pay for them. The rules are simple. Analyze the work that needs to be done before you start, and proceed slowly. Don't do more than is necessary to restore an old doll.

Finding and restoring *Ginny* or any other doll can be a rewarding experience. Who knows, even a new career as the owner of a doll hospital may come about because of your new-found interest. Many hours of pleasure are yours as another part of the great hobby of doll collecting!

E. An Identification Guide to Vogue Clothing Labels

1930s. The writing is embroidered with gold thread on white and the tag is sewn folded in the outfit. This label was used on the Just Me dolls an on the very first composition dolls.

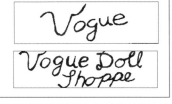

1945-46. The lettering is blue on white cotton. This label was used on composition dolls. It is folded in half and sewn into the outside back of the outfit.

Late **1940s.** This tag has white letters on a blue "ink spot" background. The tag is white cotton. This tag was used on later compositions and the first hard plastics with painted eyes. It is sewn on the outside back of the outfit.

1950-51. This label is white rayon with blue lettering. It was used on painted eye hard plastics and the first sleep eyed hard plastics that have the earlier paler finish and mohair wigs.

1952-53. This label is white rayon ribbon with blue printing. It is mostly sewn inside the outfit but is occasionally found on the outside back of the outfit. It is used on the sleep eye strung dolls.

144

1953. White rayon ribbon tag with blue print. This tag is used on the later 1953 *Ginny* dolls with dynel wigs. It is sewn inside the garment.

> ORIGINAL *Vogue* DOLLS, INC.

1954-56. This label is white rayon ribbon with black printing. It was used on the painted lash and molded lash walker dolls, It is sewn inside the outfit.

> VOGUE DOLL, INC.*
> MEDFORD, MASS. U. S.A.
> * REG. U.S. PAT. OFF.

1957- mid **1960**s. This label is white cotton with blue printing. It is sewn inside the outfit and was used on bent-knee walker dolls and the transitional doll with vinyl head and hard plastic body.

> *Vogue Dolls, Inc.*

1966- early **1970**s. This label is white cotton with blue printing. This label was used on the all vinyl *Ginny*s made in the U.S.A. It was sewn in the inside back of the garment.

> *Vogue Doll Inc.* MADE IN U.S.A.

1972. Label is paper with dark green printing. The number on the left varied. The label is sewn inside the garment and appeared on the Vogue *Ginny*s made in Hong Kong.

> 8 | MADE IN HONG KONG

1978. White cloth label with black print. It was used on the Lesney *Ginny*s with sleep eyes.

> MADE IN HONG KONG 1

1978. White paper label with red printing. This label was used on the Lesney painted eye *Ginny* from far-away lands.

> D | MADE IN HONG KONG

1981. White ribbon label with black print. This was used on the painted eye SASSON *Ginny*s. It is sewn inside the garment.

> MADE IN CHINA

1984. White ribbon label with black print. It is used on the Vogue sleep eye *Ginny*s.

> Vogue dolls, INC. © 1984

From the late 1940s to the late 1950s, there was considerable overlapping in the labels as old stock was used up by the home sewers. It is necessary to keep this in mind when trying to date a garment. Also, in the late 1940s it appears that no labels were used for a time. Instead, round gold stickers printed with "Vogue" were placed on the front of the outfit.

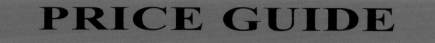

PRICE GUIDE

Price Guide Editor – Ann Tardie

1922–1937

The Vogue Doll Shoppe dressed small bisque dolls manufactured by Armand Marseille and imported to America. The dolls are 7-1/2in (19cm) tall, marked on the head "Just Me/Registered Germany" with numbers following. The earliest ones had unpainted bisque heads, followed by painted bisque and finally composition heads. All of them had slender composition bodies jointed at neck, shoulders, and hips. They had curly mohair wigs and sleep eyes. Many of the outfits were not tagged; some had labels with "Vogue" in gold on white cloth. In original clothes, the dolls are valued as follows.

Unpainted	$1,200-1,800
Painted bisque	$850 up
Composition	$500 up

These early Vogue dolls were all composition with painted features and mohair wigs. They were jointed at neck, shoulders, and hips. The earliest one (1937-1941), were marked R&B on the torso; the next ones (1942-1943) were marked "Vogue" on the head and "Doll Co." on the back of the torso. These later dolls are the most desirable as the features are more defined and the overall quality is better. Many of these early outfits are untagged and some had gold foil circles with "Vogue" printed on it which were glued to the front of the outfit.

Little Girl or Boy in original
  clothes $300
Indian Boy or Girl ....400 ea.
Cowboy or Cowgirl 375
Victory Gardeners 500
Prince Charming 400
Cinderella....................................400
Fairy Godmother 400
Hansel 375
Gretel 375
Jack 375
Jill...375
Mistress Mary 375
Mary Lamb 400
Bo-Peep 375
Peter Pan 500
Wee Willie Winkie 450
Red Riding Hood..........................425

Sunshine Babies with curved
  baby legs ....$450 up
Miss America 450
Nurse 375
Sailor 350
Naval Captain...............................350
Aviator 450
Air Raid Warden 450
Soldier 450
Civil Defense Marshall 450
Uncle Sam 550
Clown...325
Robin Hood 450
Policeman....................................375
Boys and Girls in various
  foreign costumes ....300 ea.
Brother and Sister sets.................800 up

1948-1950

These dolls are all hard plastic with painted side glancing eyes. They are jointed at neck, shoulders and hips. They have mohair wigs over molded hair. They are marked "Vogue Doll" on back of the torso. Clothes may have one of two tags: white rayon label with blue lettering "Vogue Dolls" with wavy lines above and below the lettering, or a white cotton tag with white letters "Vogue Dolls, Inc. Medford, Mass." on a blue background.

Little Girl or Boy in original clothes	$400	
Nursery Rhyme Characters	450	
Bride	400	
Groom	425	
Bridesmaid	425	
Ring Bearer	425	
Cinderella	450	
Fairy Godmother	450	
Prince Charming	450	
Crib Crowd Babies with curved baby legs	850	up

Easter Parade #24	$500	
Easter Girl #21	500	
Valentine Girl	525	
Queen of Hearts	550	
Tennis Player	300	up
Skater	350	
Brother and Sister sets	900	up
Half Century Group	1700	ea.
Extra complete outfits	200	ea.

1950-1953

All hard plastic with sleep eyes and painted lashes. They are jointed at neck, shoulders and hips. The earliest ones were the heavier hard plastic, like the painted eye dolls, with paler coloring and mohair wigs. Many of these dolls have violet or reddish brown eyes. Later ones have higher facial color, red lips and wigs of dynel or "nutex," which is a synthetic soft saran blend. Eyes are blue or brown. Tags are blue lettering on white ribbon imprinted "Vogue" or "Original Vogue Dolls, Inc."

Little Girl in original tagged clothes	$450	up
Vogue Sweetheart	475	
1950 Queen of Hearts	500	up
1950 #21 Springtime	400	
1950 #24 Easter Parade	400	
1950 Easter Bunny Crib Crowd	1,500	up
1950 Crib Crowd Babies	950	up
1951 Holly Belle	450	
1951 #32 Nan	400	
1951 #29 Tina	400	
1951 #23 Kay	400	
1951 #41 June	400	
1951 #42 Glad	400	
1951 #43 Beryl	400	
1952 Poodle Cut Pixie	600	up

1952 #33 and #34 Brother and Sister	$900	pr.
1952 #35 and #36 Brother and Sister	900	pr.
1952 #37 and #38 Brother and Sister	900	pr.

1952 TINY MISS SERIES

#39	$400	
#40	400	
#41 Poodlecut	600	

1952 KINDERGARTEN SERIES

#21	$400	
#22	400	
#23	400	

#24 Poodlecut.............................$600 up
#25 375
#26 Poodlecut.............................600 up
#27 375
#28 375
#29 375
#30 Poodlecut.............................600 up
#31 375
#32 375

1952 TINY MISS SERIES
#42 ....$400
#43 400
#44 400

1952 DEBUTANTE SERIES
#60 ....$425
#61 425
#62 425
#63 425
#64 425
#65 425

1952 FROLICKING FABLES SERIES
Julie $375
Wee Willie (Poodlecut)................600
Alice 450
Scotch 375
Indian 500
Priscilla................................450
John Alden 450
Mistress Mary............................400
Calypso..................................550
Ballet 375
Cinderella 475
Christine 375
Red Riding Hood 375
Bo-Peep 375
Mary Lamb................................450
Rodeo Girl 425
Rodeo Boy 400
Holland Girl 275
Holland Boy 275

1952 GINNY SERIES
#80 ....$375
#81 375

#85 ....$375
#86 375

1952 SPORT SERIES
Skier $375
Ice Skater 400
Roller Skater............................400
Beach 350
Fisherman 375
Tennis 375

1952 BRIDAL SERIES
Bride $375
Groom....................................375
Bridesmaid 400
1952 Tyrolean Boy and Girl........350 ea.

1952 SQUARE DANCE SERIES
#50 ....$425 up
#51 ....425 up
#52 ....425 up
#53 ....425 up
#54 Boy ....425 up

CASES AND TRUNKS
#822....................................$1,100
#823....................................1,000
#824 900
Extra Complete Outfits ....125 ea.
#840 Miniature Suitcase...............50

1953 OUTFITS WITH TALON ZIPPERS
#70 A.M.................................$375
#71 P.M. 350
#72 School 375
#73 Afternoon...........................375
#74 Party 375
#75 Stormy Weather.....................350

1953 KINDERGARTEN – AFTERNOON SERIES
#21 Linda $375
#22 Donna 375
#23 Kay 375
#24 April...............................375
#25 Connie 375
#26 Carol 400

1953 KINDERGARTEN – SCHOOL SERIES

#27 Hope $350
#28 Margie 375
#29 Tina 350
#30 Dawn 375
#31 Pat 375
#32 Nan 375

1953 TWIN SERIES

#33 Hansel $325
#34 Gretel..................................325
#35 Dutch Boy 275
#36 Dutch Girl 275
#37 Cowboy 350
#38 Cowgirl 350

1953 TINY MISS SERIES

#39 Lucy....................................$375
#40 Wanda 375
#41 June 375
#42 Glad.....................................375
#43 Beryl 375
#44 Cheryl 375

1953 GADABOUT SERIES

#45 Ballet $400
#46 T.V......................................325
#47 Roller Skater 375
#48 Beach...................................350
#49 Ski 350
#50 Ice Skater.............................375

1953 FABLE AND BRIDE SERIES

#51 Alice $400
#52 Red Riding Hood 400
#53 Bo-Peep........................... 375
#54 Mistress Mary 375
#55 Bride 325
#56 Bridesmaid 375

1953 DEBUTANTE SERIES

#60 Pamela................................$400
#61 Cathy 400
#62 Becky...................................400
#63 Karen...................................375
#64 Ginger 400
#65 Angela 375
Coronation Queen ....900 up
Black Ginny...............................1,700 up
#820 Acetate Hat Box with
    Six Hats 100
#822 Fitted Wardrobe Chest..... 950 up
#825 "Rich Aunt" Fitted
    Wardrobe Chest ....950 up
#828 "Rich Uncle" Fitted
    Red Suitcase ....950 up
#840 Miniature Showcase 75
#850 E-Z-Do Wardrobe 110

EXTRA COMPLETE OUTFITS

School & Play Outfits $100
Party Type Outfits 125
Sports Outfits 100

1954

A walking mechanism was added this year, but the dolls still have the painted lashes with sleep eyes. The wigs are dynel. The label is black print on white ribbon: "Vogue Dolls, Inc., Medford, Mass. U.S.A., Reg. U.S. Pat Off."

Doll in little girl outfit ....$325 up

THE CANDY DANDY SERIES

#51 ....$300
#52 350
#53 300
#54 350
#55 350
#56 350

MY TWIN SETS

#33 Hansel $275
#34 Gretel..............................275
#35 Dutch Boy 225
#36 Dutch Girl 225
#37 Cowboy 275
#38 Cowgirl 275

FOR FUN TIME

#45 Ballerina $300
#46 Tennis Player 275
#47 Roller Skater 275
#48 Beach 275
#49 Skier...............................275
#50 Ice Skater.......................300

FOR RAIN OR SHINE

#27 ....$275
#28 275
#29 275
#30 275
#31 275
#32 275

MY TINY MISS STYLES

#39 ....$300
#40 300
#41 300
#42 300
#43 300
#44 300

MY KINDER CROWD DRESSES

#21 ....$275
#22 275
#23 275
#24 300
#25 350
#26 350

MY FIRST CORSAGE STYLES

#60 ....$375

#61 ....$375
#62 375
#63 350
#64 375
#65 400

THE WHIZ KIDS GROUp

#70 ....$275
#71 300
#72 300
#73 300
#74 300
#75 275
Black Ginny...........................1,700 up

EXTRA COMPLETE OUTFITS:

School & Play Outfits $100
Party Outfits 110
Sport Outfits 100
#484 Fur Coat & Hat 75
#851 Set of Four Ginny
    Eyeglasses...............................50
#842 Shoe Bag and Shoes 65
#831 Ginny's Pup 250
    boxed.....................................325
#840 Miniature Suitcase...............40
#820 Hat Box with Five Hats........65
#850 E-Z-Do Wardrobe 100
#830 Ginny's Trip Mates ....225 set
#823 Unfitted Train Case.............55
#822 Fitted Wardrobe Chest........900 up
#826 Fitted Wardrobe Trunk ......900 up
#829 Fitted Weekender................900 up

1955-1956

Dolls are walkers with molded eyelashes. Wigs are made of dynel and saran. Same clothing tag as 1954.

Doll in little girl outfit ....$200 up

KINDER CROWD

#21 ....$250
#22 250
#23 250

#24 ....$250
#25 250
#26 275

GINNY GYM KIDS

#27 ....$250

#28	....	$250
#29	..................................,,,,	.,,,.250
#30	....	.275
#31	....	.250
#32	....	.250

AND AWAY WE GO

#51	....	$250
#52	....	.250
#53	....	.250
#54	....	.275
#55	....	.275
#56	....	.275

BON-BONS

#80	....	$425
#81	....	.425
#82	..................................,,,,..	.425
#83	....	.425
#84	....	.425
#85	....	.425

MERRY MOPPETS

#33	....	$250
#34	....	.250
#35	....	.250
#36	....	.250
#37	....	.250
#38	....	.250

TINY MISS

#39	....	$275
#40	....	.275
#41	....	.250
#42	....	.275
#43	....	.275
#44	....	.250

FUN TIME

#45 Ballerina	....	$250
#46 Dutch Girl	....	.225
#47 Roller Skater	....	.250
#48 Beach	....	.225
#49 Skier	....	.225
#50 Ice Skater	....	.250

BRIDAL TROUSSEAU

#60	....	$250
#61	.........,,,,,,.................	$250
#62	....	.225
#63	....	.275
#64	....	.250
#65	....	.275

CLOTHES AND ACCESSORIES

#180 Navy Coat	....	$35
#181 Black and White Check Coat	....	35
#182 Yellow Rain Slicker	....	50
#183 Velvet Coat	....	35
#184 Bunny Fur Coat	....	60
#185 2 Piece Pajamas	....	35
#186 Flowered Robe	....	30
#187 Plastic Raincape	....	25
#188 Budget Style Dresses	....	30
#831 Ginny's Pup	....	250
#840 Miniature Suitcase	....	40
#833 Parasol	....	25
#852 Extra Wigs	....	40
#821 Separate Hats	....	20-25
#872 Notepaper & Pencil	....	100
#843 Boxed Shoes & Socks	....	20
#851 Four Pair Eyeglasses	....	50
#870 Metal Stands	....	10
#910 Bed	....	75
#912 Dream Cozy Bed Set	....	75
#915 Trousseau Tree	....	300 up
#917 Rayon Quilted Puff	....	25
#920 Heart Shape Chair	....	75
#922 Wardrobe	....	60
#925 Gym Set	....	550
#845 Curlers and Cosmetic Cape	..	25
#847 Ice Skates and Socks	....	25
#848 Roller Skates	....	25
#835 Golden Locket	....	95
#836 Purse and Bead Set	....	15
#844 Set of Six Hangers	....	10
#866 Fitted Bridal Chest	....	1000 up
#860 Suitcase with Ginny & Two Outfits	....	700 up
#862 Fitted Wardrobe Trunk	......	900
#865 Holiday Fitted Wardrobe Trunk	....	900

FORMALS

#6060 ....$350
#6061 350
#6062 375
#6063 350
#6064 350
#6065 350
#6092 Nun 275

DEBS

#6070 ....$350
#6071 350
#6072 350
#6073 400
#6074 375
#6075 375

KINDER CROWD

#6021 ....$250
#6022 275
#6023 225
#6024 275
#6025 275
#6026 250

GYM KIDS

#6027 ....$250
#6028 225
#6029 250
#6030 250
#6031 250
#6032 275

MERRY MOPPETS

#6033 ....$250
#6034 250
#6035 250
#6036 250
#6037 Nurse 250
#6038 275

PLAY TIME

#6051 Dutch Girl $200
#6052 225
#6053 235

#6054 ....$225
#6055 210
#6056 Cowgirl 225

TINY MISS

#6039 ....$275
#6040 250
#6041 Clown........................275
#6042 250
#6043 275
#6044 250

FUN TIME

#6065 Ballerina $250
#6046 Drum Majorette 225
#6047 Roller Skater 250
#6048 Beach 200
#6049 Skier.........................250
#6050 Ice Skater...................250

CLOTHES AND ACCESSORIES

#6221 Shortie Pajamas $35
#6222 Red Challis Nightgown ..25
#6223 Nightgown & Peignoir ..40
#6224 Cotton Print Housecoat 25
#6180 Navy Coat, Hat,
    Pocketbook 35
#6181 Check Coat, Hat,
    Pocketbook 30
#6182 Raincoat, Bag, Umbrella45
#6183 Velvet Coat, Hat,
    Pocketbook 40
#6184 White Fur Coat, Beret,
    Muff.....................................50
#6185 Felt Coat, Headband,
    Pocketbook 30
Ginny Doll Club Certificate 60
"Hi I'm Ginny" Pin 40
#6864 Unfitted Travel Case 50
#6926 Doll House &
    Dog House ....1,500 up
#6925 Gym Set......................500
#6910 Ginny's Bed 60
#6912 Dream Cozy Set 60
#6914 Ginny's Rocking Chair 70

#6922 Ginny's Wardrobe 75
#6834 Pearls For
   Ginny & Child.....................75
#6859 Ginny Party Package ..750 up
#6860 Fitted Wardrobe Trunk550 up
#6862 Fitted Wardrobe Trunk700 up
#6865 Fitted Vacation
   Wardrobe Case ....850 up

#6866 Fitted Trousseau
   Chest................................1,500

School & Play Outfits $75
Formals 95
Skater, Skier, etc 75

1957-1962

Dolls now have bending knees. Wigs are dynel or saran. Label is blue on white "Vogue Dolls, Inc."

Doll in typical little girl outfit ..$185

#7021 185	#7055 ....$225
#7022 200	#7056 210
#7023 185	#7060 240
#7024 200	#7061 225
#7025 200	#7062 Formal 235
#7026 185	#7063 Bridesmaid..................235
#7027 185	#7064 Bride .... ,,,,,...225
#7028 185	#7065 Formal 235
#7029 185	#7070 Formal 235
#7030 185	#7071 Formal 235
#7031 .... ,,,,,,,.......185	#7072 Formal 250
#7032 Brownie 225	#7073 Formal 250
#7033 200	#7074 Formal 250
#7034 185	#7075 Formal 250
#7035 185	#7091 First Communion........275
#7036 200	#7092 Nun 200
#7037 Nurse 225	

ACCESSORIES

#7038 225	#7925 Ginny's Gym Set $550
#7039 185	#7910 Ginny's Youth Bed 55
#7040 185	#7912 Ginny's Dream
#7041 185	Cozy Set 65
#7042 200	#7914 Rocking Chair 70
#7043 185	#7920 Chest of Drawers 95
#7044 200	#7921 Table & Chairs.............95
#7045 Ballerina 185	#7922 Wardrobe 65
#7046 Drum Majorette..........200	#7837 Ginny's Apron Set 75
#7047 Roller Skater 210	#7859 Ginny's Party Package....700
#7048 Beach 185	#7860 Fitted Wardrobe Case ..600 up
#7049 Skier...........................210	#7862 Fitted Wardrobe Trunk ..750 up
#7050 Ice Skater....................200	#7863 "Gadabout" Case 85
#7051 Dutch Girl 185	#7865 Fitted Travel Trunk ....700 up
#7052 225	#7866 Fitted Trousseau Chest ..1,200 up
#7053 225	#7869 Knit Kit 60
#7054 210	

1958

Doll in typical little girl outfit ..$150	
#1110	150
#1112	150
#1113	150
#1114	150
#1115	150
#1116	150
#1117	225
#1118	150
#1119	175
#1120 Riding Habit	175
#1121	150
#1130	150
#1131 Nurse	175
#1132	175
#1134	150
#1137	165
#1138	175
#1139	150
#1140	175
#1150 Ballerina	175
#1151 Skater	185
#1152 Drum Majorette	150
#1153 Beach	175
#1154 Skier	175
#1155 Skater	175
#1156 Cowgirl	175
#1160	175
#1161	200
#1162	185
#1163	175
#1164 Bride	175
#1165 Bridesmaid	195
#1169 Nun	150
#1180 Country Fair	250
#1181 Formal	225
#1190 Formal	275

ACCESSORIES

#3690 Charm Bracelet	$95
#1690 Ginny and "Mother" Pearls	75
#1565 Miniature Suitcase	40
#1501 Ginny Sandals	30
#1553 Rainbonnet & Boots	40
#1568 Set of Four Eyeglasses	50
#1660 Ginny's Locket	85
#1535 Mittens & Ear Muffs	45
#1520 Purse & Beads Set	25
#1560 Beach Roll Set	45
#1850 Bed	50
#1852 Rocking Chair	70
#1860 Vanity	175
#1861 Table & Chairs	90
#1862 Wardrobe	65
#1880 Three Drawer Dresser	100
#1890 Ginny's Gym Set	550
#1745 Fitted Wardrobe Case	500
#1750 Weekender Package	550
#1760 Fitted Travel Trunk	675
#1534 Ginny's School Bag & Watch	100
#1590 Ginny & "Mother" Birthday Aprons	75
#1504 Headband & Gloves	25
#1531 Ice Skates	25
#1532 Roller Skates	25
#1530 Plastic Raincape	20
#1551 Separate Petticoats	20
#1550 Separate Blouses	25
Extra Complete Outfits	65

1959

Typical doll in little girl
outfit $150-175
#1253 Scandinavian 195
#1254 Oriental 210
#1255 Israelian 195
#1256 British Islander 195
#1257 Hollander....................175
#1258 Alaskan 225
#1259 Hawaiian 250
#1210 Sailor 155

#1211 Ballerina $175
#1212 Coke Outfit 195
#1213 150
#1214 150
#1215 150
#1250 Skater.........................175
#1251 Cowgirl 175
#1252 Skier...........................175
#1260 Bride 175
Extra Complete Outfits 60

1960

Typical doll in little girl outfit ..$125
Wee Imp in official Imp outfit....450 up
Wee Imp in Ginny outfit ....350 up
#1111 Riding Outfit 125
#1113 Blue Jeans 125
#1130 Cookout Outfit 325
#1132 Party Dress 150

#1151 Cowgirl $150
#1152 "Southern Belle" 250
#1160 Formal 250
#1161 Bride ....,,,,,,, .175
#1599 Book "Ginny"s
First Secret..........................175 up

1961

The majority of dolls this year had freckles and green eyes with various hair colors.

Typical doll in little girl outfit ..$150 up
#18241 Party Dress ....175 up
#18245 Bride 150

#18246 Red Velvet Frock $150
#18250 Nun 150
Extra Complete Outfits ....50 up

1962

Typical doll in little girl outfit ..$150 up
#18146 Pink Organdy &
Felt Ensemble ....175 up

1963-1965

Body is hard plastic with jointed knees and no walking mechnism. The head is vinyl with rooted hair.

Typical doll in little girl outfit ..$150 up
#18540 Snowsuit 150
#18545 Party Dress 150

#18550 Bride $150
#18551 Nun 125
#18143 Valentine Girl............150

1965-1971

Dolls are all vinyl with straight legs, no walking mechanism, and sleep eyes. Hair is rooted. Label in clothes is blue on white cotton "Vogue Dolls, Inc., Made in U.S.A."

Typical doll in little girl outfit ..$110	Nun...$75
Fairytale Land................................85	American Indian..........................110
Far-Away Lands - Except Africa 75	Ballerina 75

1971-1977

Dolls are all vinyl with straight legs, no walking mechanism, and sleep eyes. The dolls are now made in Hong Kong. Label is dark green ink on heavy white paper "MADE IN HONG KONG."

Typical doll in little girl outfit $75	Gift set with doll and
Far-Away Lands Series..................50	two extra outfits $175
Except Africa 95	

1978-1982

Dolls are all vinyl and are taller and more slender than other Ginnys. The first ones have sleep eyes, and later Sasson Ginnys have painted eyes. The 1978-1980 Far-Away Lands Series also have painted eyes and are chubbier. The 1981-1982 Far-Away Lands and International Brides have the slender bodies and painted eyes. Labels are paper and read "MADE IN HONG KONG."

1978 Sleep Eyes Ginny $25	Extra Sasson Outfits....................$10
1978 International Series 25	1978 Bed 25
Except Jamaican Girl 45	1978 Vanity...................................25
1981 Sasson Ginny.......................15	1978 Wardrobe 25
1981 International Brides..............25	1978 Desk.....................................25
1981 Far-Away Lands...................15	1978 Moped 75
Extra 1978 Outfits 10	

1984-1986

Dolls are all vinyl and use the face mold (or one similar) to the dolls made in 1963-1971. All dolls have sleep eyes and rooted hair. They are marked, "Ginny" on the head, and a star with "M.I.I. Hong Kong" on the back. Most are little girls. One notable doll is the reissue of the Coronation Queen, value is $125 up. Other dolls valued at $30-50. (See Store Specials for other information.)

1986-1993
(R. Dakin Company)

The name Ginny, Vogue Dolls was acquired by the R. Dakin Company in San Francisco in the fall of 1986. Hard plastic dolls marked: "VOGUE" DOLLS//© 1986 R. DAKIN & CO.//MADE IN CHINA."

Some groups and organizations had dolls provided to them by Dakin, which they dressed themselves, most often in approved designs.

Dolls are all vinyl and are taller and more slender than other Ginnys. The first ones have sleep eyes, and later Sasson Ginnys have painted eyes. The 1978-1980 Far-Away Lands Series also have painted eyes and are chubbier. The 1981-1982 Far-Away Lands and International Brides have the slender bodies and painted eyes. Labels are paper and read "MADE IN HONG KONG."

Specials Editions

1987 Meyer's, New Brunswick, New Jersey, Cinderella and Prince Charming 200
1988 Meyer's, New Brunswick, New Jersey, Clown 125
1989 Meyer's, New Brunswick, New Jersey, Cowgirl 100
1985 Shirley's Dollhouse, Wheeling, Illinois, Ginny Goes Country 65
1986 Shirley's Dollhouse, Wheeling, Illinois, Ginny Goes to the Country Fair 75
1987 Shirley's Dollhouse, Wheeling, Illinois, Black Ginny in Swimsuit 30
1988 Shirley's Dollhouse, Wheeling, Illinois, Santa and Mrs. Claus ....100 up
1989 Shirley's Dollhouse, Wheeling, Illinois, Sunday Best (black girl) 40
1987 Gigi's Favorite Ginny 95
1988 Sherry's Teddy Bear Ginny 95
1989 Toy Village, Lansing, Michigan, Ashley Rose 125
1987 U.F.D.C. Miss Unity (designed by Jan Quisenberry) 250
1989 U.F.D.C. Luncheon Ginny (designed by A. Glenn Mandeville) 250
1986 Modern Doll Convention Rose Queen ....250 up
1987 Modern Doll Convention Ginny at the Seashore ....95 up
1988 Modern Doll Convention Ginny's Claim...65 up
1989 Modern Doll Convention Ginny in Nashville ....75 up
1989 Vogue Doll Review Luncheon ....100 up
1988 Enchanted Doll House Ginny $150
1990 Modern Doll Convention Ginny Vacation in Orlando.......................................100
1990 Vogue Doll Review Luncheon 125
1990 Vogue Doll Club Member Special...75
1991 Vogue Doll Review Luncheon 125
1991 Little Friends of Anchorage Alaska, Alaska Ginny.......................................75
1991-1994 Modern Doll Convention Ginny dolls ....95 ea.
1992 Meyer's New Brunswick, New Jersey. Storytime Ginny.......................................75
1993-1995 Vogue Doll Review Luncheon ....75 ea.
1994 Meyer's New Brunswick, New Jersey. Celebration Ginny 95
1995 Meyer's New Brunswick, New Jersey. Ginny Loves Disney.......................................225
1996 Meyer's New Brunswick, New Jersey. Red, White, Blue Ginny.......................................75
1997 Meyer's (new location) Edison, New Jersey. Pearl Princess Ginny 75

Retired and Sold Out (regular line)

First Ballet (9505) $50-55

America's Sweetheart (6GC01)..65-100

Specials Editions

1994 Modern Doll Convention Ginny Doll 95

Ginny 95 Disney (9507) 85-90

1996 "Ginny" Disney (6DM02-SP-DIS) 85-90

Ginny at the Quay, Guys & Dolls Doll Club (SP-9701) 65-75

Ginny in Bloom, Shaker Doll Club (SP-9702) 50-55

Ginny travels to Toy Village (SP-9706)..55-65

Ahoy Ginny, Modern Doll Convention (SP-9707) 90-100

1997 Pearl Princess Ginny, Meyers (new location) Edison, New Jersey 75

Ginny the Pooh (SP-9708)..100-150

The Ginny Doll Club™
Join the club today!

1997 marked the 75th Anniversary of the Vogue Doll Company.
Join the Ginny Doll Club™ so that you don't miss a thing!

Membership includes:

♥ Four colorful issues of The Ginny Journal™

♥ The opportunity to obtain the Ginny Doll Club exclusive.

♥ Your membership card.

♥ Your membership club pin.

To become a member:

Call **1-800-554-1447**

(Use your Visa or Mastercard to charge your membership)

Or write to: The Ginny Doll Club™
1 Corporate Drive
Grantsville, MD 21536

INDEX

A

Accessories; 61, 93-94, 136-140
Africa; 85
African-American Ginny; 30, 50, 54, 104, 115, 133
Alice; 37
Alice in Wonderland;45
America's Sweetheart; 96
Angela; 41
Anniversary, Vogue's 75ᵗʰ; 112, 123
Antique Lace; 90
April; 46
Aviator; 11

B

Bakes Bread; 111
Ballerina; 57, 66, 113
Banana Split; 135
Bareback Rider; 128
Becky; 34
Beryl; 43
Bobby Soxer; 134
Bon Bons; 61
Bridal Series; 27-28, 40
Bride; 11, 64, 82
Bride & Groom; 98
Bridesmaid; 30, 35, 52
British Islander; 77
Brother Sister Series; 14, 32
Brownie; 66

C

Cabana Casual; 135
Captain; 11
Caramel Apple; 108
Car Hop; 129
Carlson, Virginia Graves; 6, 30, 49, 67, 85, 120
Carol; 30
Cathy; 46

Cheryl; 31
Christmas Dress; 72
Christmas Stocking; 140
Cinderella; 11
Clothing Packs; 119-122
Clothing labels; 144-145
Clown; 15, 70, 127
Coat; 51
Colonial Girl; 86
Communion; 71
Concert Pianist; 99
Coronation Queen; 29, 91
Cowboy & Cowgirl; 48
Country Fair; 107
Crib Crowd; 15, 17, 19, 23, 28, 32

D

Dakin, Inc.; 92-93
Dance of the Sugarplum Fairy; 131
Davy Crockett; 55
Debutante Series (Becky); 34
Debut Collection; 112, 114
Diamond Jubilee Princess; 123
Dress Me Ginny; 116-117, 119
Dutch Ginny; 62

E

Easter Bunny; 22, 134
Eskimo; 84

F

Fabulous Fifties Collection; 128-130, 134-135
Fairy Godmother; 11, 91
Fairy Tale Dolls; 11
Far Away Lands Series; 76-77, 81-82, 84
Farmer's Market Ginny; 107
Fifth Avenue Ginny; 106
First Corsage Ginny; 54
First Ballet; 113

First Communion; 132
Fitted Trousseau Chest; 75
Fitted Wardrobe Chest; 44
Formal gowns; 62, 68, 72
Freddie the Fish; 54, 138
Frolicking Fables Series; 41
Fur coat; 63, 106
Furniture; 57, 61, 87, 89

G

Geraniums Ginny; 103
Gift Set; 60, 87
Gingerbread Cookies Ginny; 109
Ginnette; 87, 91
Ginny Bunny; 134
Ginny Celebrates Collection; 132
Ginny Cooks Collection; 108-109, 111, 135
Ginny Doll Club; 63, 93, 96, 123, 128
Ginny Gardens Collection; 101-103, 133
Ginny Hits the Big Apple; 125
Ginny in Camelot; 95
Ginny Photographs Yosemite; 125
Ginny Series; 31
Ginny Sweet Shoppe; 89
Ginny Travels Collection; 97, 125
Ginny's Gym Set; 74
Ginny's Little Circus Collection; 126
Graves, Jennie; 5-6, 50, 59
Groom; 40

H

Happy Birthday Ginny; 112
Hearts & Flowers; 123
Holiday Girl; 90
Hot Cocoa; 110
Holland Boy & Girl; 41
Hula Ginny; 94

INDEX

I

Ice Cream Parlor; 131
Ice Skater; 67, 128
Indian; 83
International Brides Series; 90

J

Jamaican Girl; 86
Jan (Jill's girlfriend); 76, 79
Jeff (big brother); 76, 79
Jill (big sister); 71, 74, 79, 82
John Alden; 16
Julie; 16
June; 35, 47
Just Me; 7-8

K

Kay; 34
Kindergarten Afternoon Series; 30, 34
Kindergarten Series; 24, 26, 37, 40,42, 44

L

Lawton, Keith; 96, 98, 101
Lawton, Wendy; 96, 98-99, 101, 112
Lesney Corporation; 86, 90
Lipfert, Bernard; 10
Line Dancing; 100
Luggage; 58
Lunch at the Plaza; 105

M

Maid of Honor; 99
Mary Lamb; 45, 82
Meritus Industries; 90, 92
Minister; 11
Miss Ginny; 83-84, 92
Miss 2000; 13
Miss 1910; 13
Miss 1920; 13

Mistress Mary; 22
Music Recital; 114
My First Corsage; 51
My Kinder Crowd; 55
Myers; 91, 93

N

Nun; 67, 82
Nurse; 11
Nursery Rhyme Series; 11

O

One Half Century Group; 13
On Stage Collection; 97, 99, 131

P

Pajama Party; 135
Pamela; 43
Petunia; 102
Porcelain Ginny; 91
Pretty in Plaid; 124
Priscilla; 16
Prom Night Ginny; 130
Puttin' on the Ritz; 97

R

Rainbow Ballerina; 38
Raincoat; 77, 121
Red Riding Hood; 15, 21
Reiling, Walter; 90
Ring Master; 126
Roller Skater; 67

S

Sailor; 11
School Days Collection; 114-115, 133
Shirley's Dollhouse; 93-94
Sister; 20, 32, 47
Smith, David; 96, 98, 101, 118
Smith, Jim; 96-98, 101, 104

Smith, Linda; 4, 96, 98, 101, 104, 118
Smith, Susanne; 96, 98-99
Soldier; 11
Sparky (*Ginny*'s pup); 49, 56, 63, 73, 124
Sports Series; 25,
Square Dancer Series; 33
Stepping Out; 104
Sunday Best; 114
Sunshine Baby; 8,10
Sweetheart Ginny; 27
Sweetpea; 133

T

Tightrope Walker; 127
Tiny Miss; 25, 30, 35-36, 38, 42-43, 56
Toddles; 9, 11
Tonka; 85
Town & Country Collection; 104
Trapeze Artist; 126
Trunk; 60, 117
Twin Series; 48
Tyrolean Boy; 39

U

Uncle Sam; 11

V

Valentine Girl; 27, 59

W

Wardrobe trunk; 75
Wee Imp; 78
Wee Willie Winkie; 43, 80